BLOODAXE CO   ETS

France has been a dominant force in the development of European culture over the past hundred years. It has made essential contributions and advances not just in literature but in all the arts, from the novel to film and philosophy; in drama (Theatre of the Absurd), art (Cubism and Surrealism) and literary theory (Structuralism and Post-Structuralism). These very different art forms and intellectual modes find a dynamic meeting-point in post-war French poetry.

Some French poets are absorbed by the latest developments in philosophy or psychoanalysis. Others explore relations between poetry and painting, between the written word and the visual image. There are some whose poetry is rooted in Catholicism, and others who have remained faithful to Surrealism, and whose poetry is bound to a life of action or political commitment.

Because it shows contemporary French poetry in a broader context, this series will appeal both to poetry readers and to anyone with an interest in French culture and intellectual life. The books themselves also provide an imaginative and exciting approach to French poets which makes them ideal study texts for schools, colleges and universities.

The series has been planned in such a way that the individual volumes will build up into a stimulating and informative introduction to contemporary French poetry, giving readers both an intimate experience of how French poets think and write, and an informed overview of what makes poetry important in France.

BLOODAXE CONTEMPORARY FRENCH POETS
Series Editors: Timothy Mathews & Michael Worton

Michael Bishop is McCulloch Professor of French at Dalhousie University, Halifax, Canada. He has published widely in the modern and contemporary fields with books such as *The Contemporary Poetry of France* (1985), *Michel Deguy* (1988), *René Char: Les Dernières Années* (1990), *Nineteenth-Century French Poetry* (1993), *Contemporary French Women Poets I and II* (1995), and *Women's Poetry in France 1965-1995* (1997).

Timothy Mathews is Professor of French at University College, London. His books include *Reading Apollinaire: Theories of Poetic Language* (Manchester University Press, 1987) and *Literature, Art and the Pursuit of Decay in 20th Century France* (CUP, 2000). He has published many articles in English and French on the interactions of word and image in texts (poetry, prose, thought) and pictures (Cubism, Surrealism and after) of the 20th century. The first volume in this series, *On the Motion and Immobility of Douve* by Yves Bonnefoy, has an introduction by him.

Michael Worton is Fielden Professor of French Language and Literature at University College London. He has published extensively on contemporary French writers, co-edited *Intertextuality: Theories and Practices* and *Textuality and Sexuality: Reading Theories and Practices* (Manchester University Press, 1990 & 1993), published two books on Michel Tournier, and is now writing a book on masculinity. The second volume in the Bloodaxe Contemporary French Poets series, *The Dawn Breakers* by René Char, is introduced and translated by Michael Worton.

For further details of the Bloodaxe Contemporary French Poets series, please see pages 9 and 213-20 of this book.

BLOODAXE CONTEMPORARY FRENCH POETS: 10

SALAH STÉTIÉ

Cold Water Shielded

Selected Poems

Edited & translated by
MICHAEL BISHOP

BLOODAXE BOOKS
UNESCO PUBLISHING

BLOODAXE CONTEMPORARY FRENCH POETS: 10
Salah Stétié: *Cold Water Shielded: Selected Poems*

Original French texts © Salah Stétié & Éditions Gallimard
1973, 1978, 1979, 1980, 1983, 1984,
1987, 1992, 1994, 1995, 1998, 2000.
English translation © Michael Bishop 2000.
Introduction © Michael Bishop 2000.

ISBN: 1 85224 487 9

First published 2000 by
Bloodaxe Books Ltd,
P.O. Box 1SN,
Newcastle upon Tyne NE99 1SN.

Bloodaxe Books Ltd acknowledges
the financial assistance of Northern Arts.

UNESCO COLLECTION OF REPRESENTATIVE WORKS

UNESCO ISBN: 92 3 003580 7

Cover printing by J. Thomson Colour Printers Ltd, Glasgow.

Printed in Great Britain by
Cromwell Press Ltd, Trowbridge, Wiltshire.

CONTENTS

L'eau froide gardée

Cold Water Shielded

GENERAL EDITORS' PREFACE

The Bloodaxe Contemporary French Poets series aims to bring a broad range of post-war French poetry to as wide an English-speaking readership as possible. Other volumes in the series have been devoted to a complete, unabridged work by a poet, in order to maintain the coherence of what a poet is trying to achieve in publishing a book of poems. The translators, often poets in their own right, adopt a range of different approaches, and in every case they seek out an English that gives voice to the uniqueness of the French poems. The quality of the translations has been widely recognised: two of the titles are Poetry Book Society Recommended Translations, an award given to only four books a year translated from any language.

Each translation in the series is not just faithful to the original, but aims to recreate the poet's voice or its nearest equivalent in another language: each is a translation from French poetry into English poetry. Each book's introduction seeks to make its own statement about how and why we read poetry and think poetry. The work of each poet dovetails with others in the series to produce a living illustration of the importance of poetry in contemporary French culture.

The editors are delighted to present *Cold Water Shielded* in collaboration with UNESCO. Though the poems here are taken from a number of Salah Stétié's books, the selection builds into a coherent, unique whole with its own character and rhythms, its own echoes, and its own engagement with the leitmotifs of Stétié's thought and experience. Like the other titles in the series, this book appears with parallel French and English text; we hope this gives an intimate sense of the poet working with word and sensation, and of the translator working with text and the feel of it. The translator, Michael Bishop, has written the preface to the volume and is especially well placed to suggest how readers might approach the poetic world of Salah Stetie. The translation aims not just to be faithful to the original, but to recreate a poetic voice; the preface evokes its own sense of why we should engage with Stétié's world, and of why we read poetry and think poetry.

TIMOTHY MATHEWS
MICHAEL WORTON
University College London

9

PORTRAIT OF SALAH STÉTIÉ BY PIERRE ALECHINSKY (1997)

INTRODUCTION

'And all woods are woods of dying
According to a beauty of intellection
Within which is locked a spiritual lion'

*

'Dust is beauty of woman and dust
Is, before the cold, the dazzled splendour of man'

The Obscure Lamp of Salah Stétié

There is very much in the work of Salah Stétié that offers darting and exquisitely uncluttered access to his experience of the real. 'I wait / I follow the oxen beneath the delicate sky,' he writes in *Sixteen Veiled Words*. Such experience, however, if it can often seem sufficient in itself, unrequiring of further allegory or decoding, held simply, absolutely as a micro-event of 'the totality, with this heart' (*Cold Water Shielded*) – such experience can, nevertheless, equally be spun about on its axis, less queried than plunged dizzyingly into its simple but abyssal mystery, understood to be shot through with a strangeness Stétié ever heeds: 'Now every night being pure algebra / in the margins of that which was written / In the blazing of the reflection from the fire of the name / Burning in the sleep of the unnamed...' (*Doll Being*).

Already we can perceive the way in which Stétié's rooted, visceral, sensual poetry is caught in a net of meditation that quickly may veer to the metaphysical whilst never losing its grip upon an ethically and emotionally driven instinct that knows the indivisibility of the categories of being and its deeper discourse. 'Heart's duty,' he can call it in *Doll Being*, 'within the pensive sarcophagal / Beauty here that the tree ruptures.' It is not surprising that we rapidly discover ourselves to be in a profoundly haunting, and perhaps as Rimbaud wrote, 'haunted', poetic universe, one that relentlessly scours itself for meaning, but whose 'music', as Yves Bonnefoy would call it, is in excess of the sign's intelligibility, beyond meaning's conceptualisations and systematisations. Stétié's poems can thus at times resemble the meditations of those mystics-cum-poets (with whose culture he is only too familiar) upon the 'salty bosom [of non-being] absent from substance /... like a question or long lamp / Grown vast through the absoluteness of the air' (*Doll Being*).

11

Throughout the poetical work that is gathered and translated in this book, and indeed well beyond it in the many subtle essays and perceptive studies Salah Stétié has devoted to writers of East and West – from Rilke and Roumî, Rimbaud and Mallarmé, to Gébrane Khalil Gébrane and Badr Chaker Es-Sayyâb, and many contemporaries such as André Du Bouchet and Adonis – certain images and fascinations recur and give both coherence and complexity, continuity and intensity to an œuvre of at once vast and yet considerably focussed proportions. Thus is it that the image – at once purely metaphorical and finely concrete – of wheat may endlessly obsess. Thus is it that images of dove and eagle may intertwine their allegories, that bow, sword and lamp may constantly unfurl and redefine their symbolic pertinence, that fire and snow, tree and 'spiritual lion', desert and desire, may weave and reweave a meaning and a music, an experience and a meditation swirlingly written and rewritten from poem to poem, book to book. The question Stétié asks in *Cold Water Shielded*, 'what is there to do – or say?', should not be thought necessarily to betray some desperation, some acquiescence in the absurd: rather, for this tireless creator and cultural ambassador of so much the West has misunderstood or, wittingly or unwittingly, subverted, may we read in it the implicit answer that *everything*, always, hic et nunc, remains to be done, said, rethought, rewoven, recreated. Such metaphorical and symbolical recurrence as we have just seen to abound is, indeed, a ceaseless remaking of the world, and a music beyond the ontological circumscription of it.

The compact observations that follow seek therefore in no way to reduce or overly delimit the conceptual factors at play in a poetry seen by Stétié himself as 'ceasing to be description, nomenclature, surface inventory' and becoming rather a 'knot of forces consumed in the very act that knots them, transmuted into invisible matter, magnetic field'. At best, some paths will be traced through the opacities and the at once brilliantly revealing and blinding clarities of a remarkable œuvre wonderfully accessible, endlessly meditatable. Some paths, opening upon infinite others...

Burning, Brilliance, Opaqueness

There is, in Stétié's work, a persistent vision of the creation set afire, between tears and dove, a vision stemming from perceiving 'the sailing vessel of [the mind's] entire being [as] burning' (*Doll*

Being). Originating in a sense less of global destruction than of ceaseless exchange of energy and matter, and riding upon an intuitive experience of the revelation, the purification and what might be thought of (without moral overtone) as the natural rightness of such burning, Stétié's vision seems inalienably linked to the spectacular "hieroglyphic" combustiveness of being as it simultaneously gleams and fades. Speech, the very articulation of being it engenders – 'and us – burned with language', we read in *Sixteen Veiled Words* – clearly is caught up in this process and may be said to account, in an œuvre of such concentration and obsessiveness as Stétié's, for the 'burning of the mind to its roots' (*The Burned Other Side of Purity*) – this, however, in the perspective, quite characteristically paradoxical, recuperative, of what Stétié can term in *Cloud with Voices* the 'unburned burning' that is at the heart of being's self-consumption and self-constitution.

It is in this short, elegant last-mentioned collection that Stétié speaks of the 'light in metaphysical gestation' beaming brilliant from the ceaseless combustive creativity of what is – even 'on this black evening', as he writes in *Fragments: Poem*, 'earth and fruit, radiating'. All phenomena, events, and our experience of them can thus be seen as 'lamps precious lamps / On this burned side of purity', for their presence and the energy it emits – via us, moreover – whilst flashing, intermittent and therefore half-synonymous with a sense of opaqueness to which we need to remain alert, lie 'flashing brilliant in the burning day of the mind'. In effect, as Stétié "argues" in *The Burned Other Side of Purity* – in an argument at once elliptical, figurative and intuitive, and thus beyond rationalising reduction – 'we are here before the dazzlement / Dazzled by dazzlement'. The lamps, of world and self, that light our way also blind via the radiation of a kind of intrinsic ineffableness. 'The obscure lamp of that,' Stétié can call it, in his book of the same title, illustrated, lit up by the darkly revealing woodcuts of Raoul Ubac, the sculptor-painter who has fascinated poets such as Yves Bonnefoy and André Frénaud.

The instinctual metaphysical experience of being's burning brilliance that largely predominates in Salah Stétié's work should not be thought, however, to be so easily wrestled to the ground, nor so psychologically upbeat. Can he not write, once more in his 1992 *Burned Other Side*, of some 'entire absurd and dark lamp / In its disorder for which rags and tatters light up'? Yet, is Stétié's vision akin to that – better, those – of a Beckett, a Ionesco, a Camus? Do its roots really plunge into that neurotic and desperate mental

13

soil of a Jarry? Or might we better speak of a lingering Romantic and Symbolist struggle with *le mal* / evil, or worse, a Manichean obsession dividing being down the middle? To the latter possibility we can, despite Stétié's probable acquaintance with the Persian Manes, utter a strongly voiced *No*: light and dark tend to the inextricably unified in Stétié's ontology; and, although writers from Lamartine and Vigny to Baudelaire, Hugo and Mallarmé have left their mark on Stétié's consciousness of both the ontic – what lies at the deep heart of Being – and the formal, nothing specifically "satanical" articulates itself in the author of *Doll Being*, even via some Hugolian absorption of *le mal* within factors of goodness, love, godliness. And, if the concept of absurdity implacably calls up the poetics of many a contemporary with whom Stétié will have been necessarily familiar, no flagrant reminiscence of Beckett's *Endgame*, Ionesco's *Death of the King* or Camus' *The Myth of Sisyphus* is manifest in the work of a poet bent rather on a meditation of the 'refraction of desert and desire'.

This said, however, Stétié, in *The Earth with Oblivion*, can yet vividly conjure up the image of 'a lamp of dementia / That unravels in the sandy sand'; or, in *Burned Other Side*, he may dwell upon the purely chimerical, hallucinatory "freedom" of 'the mind whose illusion shines bright in the sky'. Yet, if, at a certain level – psychological, emotional at times, and even intellectual – dementia, absurdity and delusion may be said to veil and obscure the brilliance of our burning *ontos*, it remains paradoxically true that, for Stétié, at another level, the lamps of being continue to burn just as brightly: rags and tatters become bizarrely luminous, madness itself is illuminated, illusion, the perceptual relativities of the mind's projections, still gleam and shimmer, meta-phorical and meta-physical imagos. 'The thought / Of thought become living lamp / Rooted in the coal of being', Stétié writes, still in *Burned Other Side*.

Meaning, Being, Non-Being

As we read in *Night of Flaming Heart*, being, as we traverse it spatio-temporally and psychologically, would seem to Stétié to unfold 'beneath the unexplained roof of nights'. If illusion seems possible within its very illumination, and if confusion, fusion and teeming paradox seem to reign in the equations of "absurdity" and concomitant revelation, can we be surprised when meaning appears recessed, ever inaccessible within us and without? Not that we should see this indecipherability, this indeterminacy, as a problem, a threat experienced by Salah Stétié. On the contrary, it is perhaps rather to 'the trees of my issue before meaning', as he puts it in *Inversion of Tree and Silence*, that Stétié turns, not to seek intelligible intellectualisation, but to experience being's meaning as available *before* any rationalisation of it. When he exclaims 'Oh sparrowhawk irradiating the god of meaning', in the same book, Stétié surely holds in his mind's eye a vision of being's meaning, at once visceral and mystical, far beyond all compulsion to conceptualise reductively. It is in this light that we may best read recurrent and characteristic declarations to the effect that 'of no meaning is meaning – called meaning' – declarations that repeatedly call our attention to the profound mystery of what, in *Eagle Dove*, Stétié terms 'the immense-purposed air', a mystery beyond stable decoding yet nonetheless real, meaning beyond our verbalisation of meaning, as well expressed as 'no-meaning' as in any other way.

Being, thus, for Stétié, may be sensed and articulated, as he puts it in *Cloud with Voices*, 'by immanence and ideation', by a double process whereby 'presence' may come to dwell within us and psychic or mental activity may work with such 'in-dwelling' via the intellect and a fluid intuition buoying up the latter – for 'only blind blind men believe in theories, in theorems' (*Reading of a Woman*). If, in fact, a remark such as this last one has, read in its context, overtones that appear more socio-political than strictly ontological, it remains important to remember that, for this poet-diplomat, no real distinction between the social and the spiritual, the concrete and the psychical or meta-physical yields a satisfactory sense of our being-in-the-world. 'No-being' and being remain interlocked, no doubt synonymous, just as 'no-fire' lies within fire, or vice versa, like 'snow asleep in snow'. It is not just a matter of mortality and destruction – or even subsequent survival – of what we call (our) being, moreover. When Stétié speaks of what is, 'grassily in the extinction of the grass', the equation he draws up manifestly interweaves elements and states that may seem mutually exclusive but which are not. What, in *Doll Being*, is called the 'theatre of empty form / Like a daughter of harmony awaiting / Fulfilment', may just as easily be seen from the other perspective of 'seizure here through figuration / Before the having of no assumed form'. Being and having, nothingness and emptiness, figuration and (non-)assumption, these, and other, concepts are the dancing, swirling structures that would endlessly seek to image, via *felt* aporia and paradox, the 'face [of being] / Attached to grassy dew / Then the dew withdrawn, and the face' (*Inversion of Tree and Silence*). Stétié's experience of 'the earth won over / By the angel, oh undressed in a substance / Of no earth' clearly defies all but sympathetic, what Jean-Pierre Richard would term intersubjective, intuitive analysis. For if the figures upon the page allegorise and symbolise, what can never be adequately rationalised, but upon which all, for Stétié, rides, is 'the unfigured, the master of the lamp' (*Inversion*). And, lest we are tempted to read into these latter words a poetics of some dismissive transcendence, it is useful to reaffirm here that the fascination with the 'no-wheat of wheat' always remains, crucially, vitally, for Stétié a penetration of immanent experience of the 'ambiguous earth', a shaking, merely, yet splendidly and searchingly, of the 'rags of strength of the mind' (*Inversion of Tree and Silence*). The meaning of being/no-being may lead Stétié, as he writes in *Fragments: Poem*, to pursue some ultimate designation of 'the direction of no-direction / of no-face with / The mirror of no-mirror', but he knows such designation itself to be intrinsically 'null', haunted by the very problematics, or mystery, he tracks, the enigma of some 'viduity of the void' obsessively filtering into ideation's tussle with immanence. 'No-poetry of earth crying out / Poetry of no-poetry crying out'...

Brokenness, Knottedness, Absoluteness

If, in the context of the tensions and paradoxical inseparability of being and no-being, Stétié's imagination is drawn to project a certain poetics of damage, or what Bonnefoy terms 'imperfection', we are perhaps not surprised. The 'broken violins / Burning away with that which was', as Stétié writes in *Burned Other Side*, need not however be seen as signs of social or ethical, aesthetic or emotional collapse and disintegration. Not only does Stétié's poetry resist any such appropriation, but for him, as indeed for Bonnefoy for whom 'imperfection is the summit', being's very exquisiteness, its beauty and strange, at times perplexing mystery, caught up as they are in mortality's flow which is simultaneously a Michaux-like 'emergence/ resurgence', generate an equipollence, a sense even of the *equivalence*, of the broken and the unbroken, the damaged and the perfect. The experience and conception, in Stétié, of what he calls *éclats* ('splinters of light') thus unify the imagination of the fragment, the splinter, that which bursts asunder, and an imagination predicated on the brilliant light released via this sundering and constituting simultaneously a locus, an event, a mode of being quite contrary to any poetics of pure destruction. That 'great and brittle eagle of grass above' which Stétié evokes in *Inversion of Tree and Silence* may be seen as part of his perception, in the same book, of 'pure externalness / Rooted in breakage and in feint', and indeed there is clearly here a relaying of the experience of being's vulnerability, its temporal dimension, its apparent precariousness seen through blinkered rationality. But, of course, Stétié is precisely a poet refusing the very real temptation of our often presumptuous modern reductiveness. In that environment, being's experience can only be seen as 'feint', that is not really seen at all, or only via some process of seeing akin to Rimbaud's – with its bold, intuitive forays into the psyche's veiled vastness. 'Funereal *and unfunereal* splintering of lines / Gathered into a beauty,' Stétié finely writes in *Fragments: Poem* (my emphasis). A brokenness that is equally a no-brokenness, we might say, adopting Stétié's own lexicon.

For, in effect, what we may call, again following Stétié's lead, the absoluteness of the mortal is shot through with its own relativity, its shimmering otherness. A whole poetics of invertibility in Stétié's poetry leads, seemingly inevitably, to a high and persistent consciousness of all that is knotted, bound tightly, inextricably together despite signs of fragmentation, degradation, brokenness. Absoluteness comes thus to be felt, not as that largely dreamed symbolist construction of the ideal, but as a place/'no-place' (as a Bernard Noël or a Jacques Dupin might write, though with differing optics) where the compacted kernel of being's mystery and meaning may unknot its sheer mortality at the same time as the latter's relativity continues to re-knot itself in that 'metaphysical gestation' already evoked by Stétié in *Cloud with Voices*. Stétié's perceived-intuited 'absoluteness of the air' – or of any phenomenon or moment here and now – seems then to pulse and throb, rhythmically, paradoxically thrusting rationally polarised experience and concept into a space beyond duality. In *Cold Water Shielded* he speaks of a 'desire to be simplified / Like a ladder of imagination returning / In joy to the wood of its intrinsicalness'. Yet Stétié knows, whether what is at stake is primary experience or writing and the written – 'the book, broken, indeterminate / Like absolute theatre', we read in *Inversion of Tree and Silence* – that the simple is always the complicated, the shattered, just as the opposite is true, and that 'absoluteness' embraces both these conditions, concepts, experiences as one, as a "unified field". The wonderful poem from *Fragments: Poem*, 'The heart is naked...', comes as close as one might hope to gathering much of the above into one equally unified expressive knot, ceaselessly tying and untying itself, like so many '[transparent dice] of no-dying being dying'.

Love, Violence, Divineness

The idea that things, concrete phenomena but also all that accompanies the physical, are there 'for our love', as he affirms in *Cloud with Voices*, can bear some emphasis if we are to grasp fully the import of Stétié's poetics. 'Lovers', he argues in *Doll Being* are always 'more refined than ash / With its arid equations, their stinging nettle'. And such emotion and vision are understood to persist, to be all the more pertinent in their persistence, despite the seeming ephemeralness of love's gesture: 'And our love oh my love is snow' (*Burned Other Side*); despite, too, what in the latter book Stétié can term 'this most poor side of love / Within its odour of urine and jasmine'; and despite what may at times appear to be the signs of an exchange between self and world, self and other, predicated rather on a symbolics of violent, aggressive and counter-aggressive gesture (sword, bow, eagle, fire, tears and so on).

As with poets such as René Char and Jacques Dupin, however, the poetics of love and that of "violence" are subtly and delicately fused, this in accordance with a broad tendency to see experience as a unified, complexly paradoxical phenomenon where equipollence, correspondence and interwovenness "deconstruct" our myths of opposition, category and function. Certainly, Stétié's work seems bent on the 'sav[ing of] spirit' by non-abusive means, and certainly he can be utterly explicit in regard to the disfiguration of love, of man's love in particular: *The Earth with Oblivion* heaps 'sorrow upon this man and sorrow, and sorrow and sorrow / Upon all of this man with his sex of violence!' Such a man's love, knotted to the point of some tight invisibility, has led to so much pain, to so much isolation, deprivation, ignorance – the terms are Stétié's and can be commonly observed – that he has found himself so often 'deliver[ed] up to angelic coarseness'. But it is here that Stétié's "deconstructive", better recuperative, vision kicks in: no accusatory binge, finally, rather a return to the angelical (still) within the ruinous and the perverted, to the positive pole of a psyche only apparently subverted and short-circuited by its "negative" pole. 'Angel, he keeps vigil in the midst of his cats', Stétié caressingly writes of the same man in the same book. But, in effect, larger redefinitions are never far way and, in *Reading of a Woman*, a book never shying away from human ideological and gestural contradiction, Stétié will not hesitate to speak of 'violence, central kernel of life, itself pulpy about this pebble'. If the metaphor here is evocative of certain maladies, it is also clear that Stétié sees human action as ambivalently bound up in a use of energy whose ends and designations

– from love to violence, innocence to degradation – whilst symbolically distinct, may be inextricably unified – so quickly tipping over one into the other, so quickly disfigured, so ever possibly transfigured. No wonder Stétié can give us such strange meldings as 'beautiful bleeding', for the ever spilled, ever physically absolute 'blood' of things is, for him, mystically entrusted with 'the closed flower of being' (*Fragments: Poem*).

Such embrace of duality, compressing it into a oneness our contemporary sociologies and psychologies find difficult to contemplate, Stétié will experience, both viscerally and conceptually, as a 'divineness' beyond all doctrinal and ideological attachment. 'The straight motionlessness of a flame / shut up within itself like the idea of God' may spark his intuition (*Cold Water Shielded*); or Stétié, at once telluric and visionary, may conjure the 'God of ants in the redness / Of a land   God of lamb lovely / At the gates burst asunder' (*Cloud with Voices*). It is not, let it again be stressed, that Stétié loses sight of the manifest signs of a disabling of the 'angelical' and the 'divine'. But Stétié is not about to succumb to the temptations of 'the lost neighbour / Listen[ing] to a fire taking: / Negation'. Certainly – and this is crucial in his work – the divine fuses with what we have seen him call in *Cloud with Voices* 'the viduity of the void', 'the null / Nullness'; for 'the whirlwind of forces' which Stétié sees at play in the complex but *intuitable* equations of being and no-being 'cloth[e] God in great flowers of nullness' – flowers that continuously expropriate our conception of the divine while endlessly allowing for a fluid reappropriation thereof. A reappropriation, yet, that asks no more than that be seen, still, the feasible, half-forgotten, bloodily luminous 'goddesses of summer in the clouds' (*Burned Other Side*).

Speech, Writing

If Salah Stétié's persistent meditation on the nature of speech, language and writing is in line with the often perceptibly self-reflexive character of much modern and contemporary French poetry since Mallarmé and Rimbaud, it remains a meditation that is at once distinctive, complexly and intensely metaphorical, intimately bound up with the larger ontological concerns whose pertinence I have sought rapidly here to outline. Take, for instance, the conclusion of one of the earlier poems of *Doll Being*, where Stétié argues that, 'image having withdrawn, speech / Delivers its wheat to limpid birds / Stealing dawn from the keepers of running waters /

Before erasure in writing'. We might, not unreasonably, sketch out from this a poetics of speech involving, firstly, a deletion or retraction of 'image' (optical rather than figurative); secondly, a giving (back) of (verbal) substance to the phenomena from which speech seems to have arisen; and, thirdly, a puzzling, even disturbing (though Stétié shows calm and confidence, a kind of matter-of-factness) 'erasure' of possibly both being and speech via 'writing', in the written text. However, all this seems feasible interpretation, it remains hypothetical, ever deconstructed by the semantic and referential, not to say the conceptual, ellipses that allow it. A later poem from *Doll Being* authorises similar conjectural equations, whilst again, simultaneously, untying them by its own evacuation through metaphor of the banally analytic:

> Like a violin brought to its pure wood
> When the splendour of being turns about
> For a moon of dust and foliage
> Ornamented with the luxury of death,
> Is speech. It gives of its embers
> To the son born to it black wheat of the world:
> (Of what sun its gospel, in what language?)
> – Doe of the grass, bring love to my heart

Here, we may be inclined to conclude: (1) that speech, like (but already our rational montage skids to one side) that instrument and thing that we call a violin, attains to some purer (poetical?) intrinsicalness (of itself? of being?); (2) that this very process entails a 'turning about' (an inversion? a reversal? a versing?) of being (giving the latter a lunar brilliance, half-cosmic, half-dead?); (3) that speech, thus conceived as ash and ember, gives birth to, somehow creates (though it is not alone in this creation) – via the residual heat of its embers that repotentiate, re-illumine, rekindle – what Stétié terms (4) 'black wheat of the world': worded substance, substance-of/via-language?, that other world of language, with its own, unidentified 'sun', with its indeterminate credo underpinning it, with the question hanging over it: what *is* the language that words speak? Finally, the poem would seem to sweep aside all such conjecture in a return to being (albeit via language, metaphor) and the primacy of love, of a loving intuition of being's meaning – or, not even that, but merely the primacy of the loving experience of what is.

That the poet – with his or her swirling intuitions, constructions and deconstructions – is, as again *Doll Being* puts it, 'stretched out in writing', becomes all too clear from the above. But it remains that language, for Stétié, never ceases 'speaking of lamp'. 'The Song is bow', as he puts it in *Inversion*: that violently symbolic means of piercing and sundering being reminiscent of Char, so that light may flow therefrom. If, as we have seen, poet and reader may be 'burned with language', this is the risk and the fiery intensity that all articulation exposes one to. It can lead to a profound questioning of the latter, as we saw in *Cold Water Shielded*: 'What is there to do – or say?' It can lead equally to feelings of absence despite the strange hospitable-ness of language's 'turnings' in the midst of much that dismays: the poet as 'the guest of verses / Upon this versant in the inferno of appearances'. Or Stétié, not unlike Jacques Dupin, may dwell upon the fragile 'spideriness of speech', the vulnerability – despite the patience, the intricacy, the marvel – of the webs it tirelessly and lovingly spins – though to what end, when all is said and done, do we not hear asked: to none or to all? Moreover, there should be no surprise if, in the case of a poet privileging, with Bonnefoy, presence over figuration, ever returning to the love of the 'doe of grass' from the prestige of language's articulation of such love, we find Stétié writing, already in *Fragments: Poem*, of 'tree in the name of tree desiring / the end of naming and beginning of tree'.

If language can give us so much, Stétié seeks then never to forget that its nomination veils and masks, *turns away from* and not just *towards*, being. Thus can he, along with the tree, find himself at times serenely, even joyously, 'awaiting the promised reduction / Of name which is name behind name / With which name too will be erased' (*Burned Other Side*). This, of course, in the face of the very great œuvre, the teeming thought, speech and writing on which it rides, which, paradoxically, *do not lie in opposition* to the strange dream of no-nomination, of unnamedness that ever haunts Stétié. When he writes in the same book that, for the human being, 'the violin of what [s]he is is his[/her] triumph', it is certain that a vast ontological perspective gives deep splendour to his vision. Yet part of this splendour remains writing's tussle with being, the supple, unstable and so often exquisitely beautiful music (wo)man's 'violin' can, remarkably, at times seemingly against the odds, produce. Let s/he who doubts such splendour of speech conceived as a precarious yet powerful celebration of our being-in-the-world, read any of the poems that follow. Occasional stanzas carry over, refrain-like, from one collection to another. Small variations in the rendering of such stanzas reflect my view of the shifting, relative and ever alive nature of translation.

MICHAEL BISHOP
Queensland, Nova Scotia
& *Canterbury, England*

Selected Bibliography

SALAH STÉTIÉ: **Poetry**

L'eau froide gardée / Cold Water Shielded (Paris: Gallimard, 1973).

Fragments: Poème / Fragments: Poem (Paris: Gallimard, 1978).

Obscure lampe de cela / Obscure Lamp of That (Remoulins: J. Brémond, 1979; 1994).

Inversion de l'arbre et du silence / Inversion of Tree and Silence (Paris: Gallimard, 1980).

L'être poupée / Doll Being (Paris: Gallimard, 1983).

Colombe aquiline / Eagle Dove (Paris: Gallimard, 1983).

Nuage avec des voix / Cloud with Voices (Saint-Clément-la-Rivière: Fata Morgana, 1984).

Lecture d'une femme / Reading of a Woman (Saint-Clément-la-Rivière: Fata Morgana, 1987).

L'autre côté brûlé du très pur / The Burned Other Side of Purity (Paris: Gallimard, 1992).

La terre avec l'oubli / The Earth with Oblivion (Paris: Éditions des Moires, 1994).

La nuit du cœur flambant / Night of Flaming Heart (Paris: Éditions des Moires, 1994).

Seize paroles voilées / Sixteen Veiled Words (Saint-Clément-la-Rivière: Fata Morgana, 1995).

Éclats / Splinters of Light (Charleville-Mézières: Flache, 1995).

'Jardin de l'Un' / 'Flambeaux de la Rivière' (Charleville-Mézières: Flache, 1995; Paris: Éditions Unesco/Imprimerie Nationale, 1998).

Fièvre et guérison de l'icône / Fever and Recovery from the Icon (Paris: Éditions Unesco/Imprimerie Nationale, 1998).

SALAH STÉTIÉ: **Interviews**

La parole et la preuve, with Michel Orcel, Najmuddine Bammate, Jean-Marie Le Sidaner, Luc Norin, Nathalie Brillant, Yves Namur, Sylvie Bourgoin, Olivier Apert, Marie Ginet, Richard Millet, Daniel Leuwers, Béatrice Bonhomme (Saint-Nazaire: Éd. MEET, 1996).

Sauf Erreur, with David Raynal & Franck Smith (Grigny: Paroles d'Aube, 1999).

SALAH STÉTIÉ: **Prose**

Les porteurs de feu (Paris: Gallimard, 1972).
André Pieyre de Mandiargues (Paris: Seghers, 1978).
La unième nuit (Paris: Stock, 1980).
Les sept dormants au péril de la poésie (Louvain: Éditions Leuvense Schrijversaktie, 1991).
Lumière sur lumière ou l'Islam créateur (Le Revest-les-Eaux: Cahiers de l'Égaré, 1992).
Rimbaud, le huitième dormant (Saint-Clément-la-Rivière: Fata Morgana, 1993).
L'interdit (Paris: Corti, 1993).
Le nibbio (Paris: Corti, 1993).
Réfraction du désert et du désir (Paris: Babel, 1994).
Liban pluriel (Paris: Naufal-Europe, 1994).
L'ouvraison (Paris: Corti, 1995).
Hermès défenestré (Paris: Corti, 1997).
Le vin mystique (Saint-Clément-la-Rivière: Fata Morgana, 1994).

Selected further reading on Salah Stétié

Nathalie Brillant: *Salah Stétié: une poétique de l'arabesque* (Paris: L'Harmattan, 1992).
Mohammed Boughali: *Salah Stétié, un poète vêtu de terre* (Paris: Publisud, 1996)
Paule Plouvier and Renée Ventresque: *Itinéraires de Salah Stétié* (Paris: L'Harmattan, 1996).
Salah Stétié, 33 papers selected from international conferences held at Cerisy and Pau, ed. Daniel Leuwers & Christine Van Rogger-Andreucci (Pau: Presses de l'Université de Pau, 1997).
Yves Bonnefoy: 'Deux langues mais une seule recherche', in *Fièvre et guérison de l'icône* / Fever and Recovery from the Icon (Paris: Éditions Unesco/Imprimerie Nationale, 1998).
Giovanni Dotoli: *Salah Stétié: Le poète, la poésie* (Paris: Klincksieck, 1999).
Béatrice Bonhomme: *Salah Stétié en miroir* (Amsterdam/Atlanta: Rodopi, 2000).

COLD WATER SHIELDED

de L'eau froide gardée (1973)

De cela qui s'écrit je ne
Sais rien
– La parole est dressée dans le manque d'air

Vulnérable et nue et la
Douleur de son épée sur les fils
Liés et déliés selon leur mort

L'un après l'autre désencombrés
Elle les admet à son partage
Et leur donne un sein sauvage et réservé

*

Je salue la jeunesse de la lumière
Sur ce pays de grande chasteté
Parce que ses femmes sont fermées

Elles ont des ailes croisées sur la poitrine
Pour protéger le cœur ardent des hommes
L'amour aux cils baissés l'a circoncis

– Qui sauvera ce pays du martèlement
Des soldats qui s'avancent sous un triomphe
Pour arracher l'eau froide gardée – et la prendre ?

*

from Cold Water Shielded (1973)

Of that which is written I know
Nothing
– Speech is drawn up in airlessness

Vulnerable and naked and the
Pain of her sword upon the threads
Bound and unbound according to their death

Disencumbered one by one
She admits them to her apportionment
And gives them a wild and guarded bosom

*

I greet the youth of light
Over this land of great chasteness
Because its women are closed

Their wings lie crossed upon their breasts
To protect the ardent hearts of men
Circumcised by low-lidded love

– Who will save this land from the hammering
Of soldiers advancing beneath some triumph
To tear out cold water shielded – and possess it?

*

Rivière ma lumière
Douce déshabillée
Sur toi il y a le ciel qui est fort
C'est l'autre ciel : non pas le ciel d'éponge bleue
– Le ciel d'éponge bleue a des bustes qui fondent

C'est l'autre ciel fermé comme une lampe
Inaltérable avec dans sa verrerie
La droite immobilité d'une flamme
Close avec soi comme l'idée de Dieu

Mais toi va ton chemin douceur sous le ciel fort
Épuise nos secrets bleu vide et puis
Unis, amour, l'image avec le corps
Donne une fête à toute feuille ici qui tremble
– Avant l'arrivée des fillettes, et leur blessure

*

Le texte est de croissant sur des brisures
De cicatrices sur ces cristaux aigus
Qu'un ciel couvre de ciels arrachés ou figures
Jusqu'à l'obscur œillet qui respire

Paysage à la destruction de l'épaule
À ce bois contenu par la lune
Quand cela bat dans l'arbre et s'embrouille avec colère
Et d'aile, d'un éclat, fait la mer trop grande

– Où allons-nous, doux époux ?

Alors vient la femme avec étoiles ici et jambes
        et vraie menthe
Et lignes pour le vent l'assoupir avec plis
        dans ses beaux linges
Allume un ongle de miroir à la nuit où ses doigts
        s'éteignent
Afin que l'oiseau casse et tombe dans les chambres
        du monde

*

River my light
Soft undressed
Above you is the sky that is strong
It is the other sky : not the blue-sponged sky
– The blue-sponged sky has melting figures

It is the other sky closed like a lamp
Unalterable within its glass
The straight motionlessness of a flame
Shut up with itself like the idea of God

But go your way softness beneath the strong sky
Exhaust our empty-blue secrets and then
Joined, love, image with body
Rejoice in each leaf here that quivers
– Before the young girls come, with their wounds

*

The text is crescent-like over scarry
Cracks over sharp crystals
That a sky covers with skies torn free or figures
Down to the obscure carnation that breathes

Landscape of shoulder's destruction
Of this wood contained by moon
When things flap in the tree and confuse in anger
And a-wing, with a flash, have the sea racing

– Where are we going, gentle husband ?

Then comes woman with stars here and legs
        and real mint
And lines for the wind lulling it with folds
        in her fine linens
Lights a mirroring nail to the night in which her
        fingers die away
So that the bird snaps and falls into the rooms
        of the world

*

Dévotion à celle
De nul corps tournoyant
Les mains pâles et sûres

Aiguë
Donnant un sein
Aux arbres et aux bêtes

Et qui dressée au seuil
Attend d'une fatigue
Le début de la cendre

D'un couteau
Elle coupe
Le fruit – jusqu'à la mer

*

Les quais de marbre aux fontaines de l'eau
Sont allumés d'un grand glacé désir
D'être quais de soleil éternel pour
Sauver le feu devenu noir ici

Oh sur l'église sortie du souvenir
Et retournée en destruction avec des cris
Le cœur se brise attaqué d'une froide
Fleur éclatée sur le ciel d'ombre vide

Mais le feu flambe au poing de jeunes femmes
Marcheuses sûres de glaciers tremblants d'air
Et qui vont jusqu'au bord de mourir, si
Ne les retient le génie noué aux ailes

*

Devotion to her
Of no body spinning
With pale and certain hands

Acute
Offering her breast
To trees and beasts

And who erect upon the threshold
Awaits with a tiredness
The commencement of ash

With a knife
She cuts
The fruit – through to the sea

*

The marble wharves with their fountains of water
Are lit with a great icy desire
To be wharves of eternal sun to
Save the fire here become black

Oh above the church emerged from memory
And spun about into destruction with screams
The heart breaks assaulted by a cold
Flower burst open across the empty-shadowed sky

But fire flares up in the fist of young women
Sure walkers of trembling glaciers of air
And going to the very rim of dying, but
For the genius knotted within their wings holding them back

*

Sous quels murmures d'eau de quelle pierre
Aux doigts étroits et froids sous les murmures
L'homme s'arrête à la caverne appelée Cœur
Son propre cœur parmi les plantes ?

Il voit d'abord les cristaux dans les arbres
Se renverser en beaux chariots qui brûlent
Avant de tendre la main vers cette eau d'eau
Comme le corps qui s'est déshabillé

Va-t-il toucher cette robe qu'à la pierre
Le temps arrache en désordre et qu'il emporte
Sous de grands nœuds de songe sur le monde
Très loin de l'homme au front pierreux limpide ?

*

Celle aux yeux clairs jusqu'au lac
Qui d'une flamme aiguë se déguise
Je lui donne la fixité du givre en fleur
Et dans des paumes pauvres l'identité

Elle est habile en oiseaux figurés
En lèvres déchirées divinement
En éclat avec le double sein
Qui la fait chaude dans la région des planètes

Elle a des amitiés d'or sombre et d'hommes
Et des genoux de soumissions nombreuses
Quelquefois elle est seule : le soir
Aggrave ses habitudes précieuses

*

Beneath what water whisperings of what stone
With cold and slender fingers beneath the whisperings
Man stops at the cave called Heart
His own heart amongst the plants?

He sees first the crystals in the trees
Thrown back into fine chariots that burn
Before proffering a hand to this water of water
Like the body that has shed its clothes

Will he touch this robe that in disorder
Time snatches from stone and carries off
Beneath great clumps of revery across the world
Most far from man of limpid stony brow?

*

To her of eyes clear to the very lake
That in acute flame is masked
I give the fixedness of flowering frost
And in palms of poverty, identity

She is skilled in figured birds
In lips torn divinely
In bursting brilliance with her double bosom
That gives her warmth in the vicinity of planets

She has dark-gilded and male friendships
And knees of endless yieldings
At times she is alone : evening
Complicates her precious habits

*

L'iris de feu perce les eaux serrées
De ce visage accompli sur la rive
Celle qui prie pour sauver la plus rouge
Bouche inconsolée de sa blessure

Plus bas la courbe de l'épaule et les deux seins
Allant au monde et doux d'être sans mère
Avec le drapeau d'une paix avant la guerre
Et le buisson de Dieu, tables ardentes

Plus bas le pain des cuisses pour les anges
Et leur faim pure. Et l'armée des orteils
Qui vont au mal. L'épée qui la divise :
– Ce tourbillon d'herbe et de sang

*

Qu'il soit dit que nous serons sauvés
Dans notre vie et dans son ombre double
À cause d'une échelle simple qui
Connaît d'ici les bois de l'autre rive

Ô tête fraîche et brûlante dans le temps
Je te vois fraîche en un jardin gardé
Et je te vois brûlante en un jardin
Gardé par une épée

Ce sont deux jardins pour une tête
Dont le désir est d'être simplifiée
Comme une échelle imaginée qui retourne
Joyeusement au bois de sa nature

*

The iris of fire pierces the tight waters
Of the face accomplished by the water's edge
She who prays to save the reddest
Mouth unconsoled in its wound

Below the shoulder's curve and her breasts
Going to the world and soft in their motherlessness
With the flag of a peace before war
And God's bush and burning tables

Below yet the bread of thighs for angels
And their pure hunger. And the army of toes
Destined for harm. The sword that divides her in two
– This whirlwind of grass and blood

*

Let it be said we shall be saved
In our lifetime and in its twice-shadowedness
Because of a simple gangway that
Knows from here the woods of the other bank

Oh cool head burning in time
I see you cool in a shielded garden
And I see you burning in a garden
Shielded by a sword

Two gardens there are for a mind
Whose desire is to be simplified
Like a ladder of imagination returning
In joy to the wood of its intrinsicalness

*

L'air est parti avec les mouches.
Demeure un froid : la blanche aux seins
Les donne aux formes des chevaux dans une chambre
Où dorment leurs naseaux forts et tués.

Le marbre est fort. Le dieu – sorti.
Il tourne seul au-dessus des prés sombres.
Ici laissant dans un arrachement
Son bras immense.

Le bras déraciné d'un dieu. Que faire – ou dire ?
La parole blesse au talon le sang des hommes
Surgis sur l'éclat des murs. Dehors il y a
– Debout, ses oreilles noires, Isis.

*

Par le lieu qui a prêté son nom au livre
Par l'amande limpide
Volée aux dieux

L'égarement brûle les cils de la mer –
Et quel instant de nul instant se brise
Contre des genoux morts ?

Oh quel genou sur ce cœur
Dans la violence déployée frangée de plumes
Le tout, avec le cœur /

*

The air has left with the flies.
A coldness remains : the breasted woman in white
Suckles the shapes of horses in a room
Where strong and massacred their nostrils slumber on

Strong is the marble. The god – departed.
He moves about alone above the dark meadows.
Leaving here in a great wrenching
His vast arm.

The uprooted arm of a god. What is there to do – or say ?
Speech wounds the bloodied heel of men
Surging over the bright-shivered walls. Outside there is
– Standing high, her ears black, Isis.

*

By the place that has lent its name to the book
By the limpid almond
Stolen from gods

Bewilderment burns the filaments of the sea –
And what instant of no instant is broken
Against dead knees ?

Oh what knee upon this heart
In the deployed violence feather-fringed
The totality, with this heart /

*

L'idée est en feu sur la montagne
L'eau s'est égarée

Ce qui longtemps traverse
Est cheval de vertèbres
Définition d'insecte

Sous l'air la montagne s'est couchée
En fourmi absolue

*

The idea is on fire upon the mountain
The water has gone astray

What is long in traversing
Is horse of vertebrae
Definition of insect

Beneath the air the mountain has lain down
Like an ant absolute

*

L'endroit d'une vipère près du cœur
Sous les violences du laurier et sa violence
Alliée à l'apparue des rosées

Une main consumée sous la feuille et les doigts
Cherchant l'antiquité brûlante de la lune
Domiciliée dans la maison des derniers arbres

Vipère contre, la jambe la plus belle
Descendra nuitamment tous les chemins de l'herbe
– Et seulement la main raffinée d'écriture

*

Le loup est dans le soir et dans les amandiers
Beau visage du loup contre ma jambe
Ma brune femme, racine rassurée

Mais qui dira le nom funèbre de ma jambe
Dans la Maison de l'Être quand une main
Avancera l'extrême lampe

Vers l'autre lampe et l'autre sœur
Semblable et l'autre jambe
Veuve dans le non-nommé crépuscule ?

*

The place of a viper by the heart
Beneath the laurel's violences and its violence
Wedded to the manifest dew of dews

A hand consumed beneath the foliage and fingers
Seeking the burning antiquity of the moon
Lodged in the house of final trees

Viper close by, the loveliest leg
Will nightly go down every path of the grass
– And only the hand refined in writing

*

The wolf is in the evening and in the almond-trees
The wolf's fine face against my leg
My dark-hued woman, rooted, reaffirmed

But who will say the funereal name of my leg
In the House of Being when a hand
Holds forward the extreme lamp

Towards the other lamp and the other sister
Like her and the other leg
Widowed in the not-named dusk?

*

La lumière sur les arbres
Allonge le prénom et courbe l'air des chambres
Où voyage en immobilité fraîche un dieu de cendre

Il fatigue un verger de fers /
Trahis / bientôt sauvés par l'oiseau frère
Qui laisse au sommet du bond ses ailes brillantes

Une épousée est dans une ombre vide
Ses seins d'eau sont longue poussière nocturne
Ses doigts gardés par des vivants d'automne

*

Franchies et pures, maisons
D'antiquité friable / celles
Traversées de seuils froids, leurs
Visages à la brillante poussière

Puis retirés dans la
Solitude aveugle de l'éclat-pollen. Le
Corps de plusieurs nuits jeunes, allégé de
Vides grappes –

Puis l'éternité de chèvre
Broutera le peu. Le jour. Le sein
Ira / brûlant.

*

The light on the trees
Gives length to the first name and bends the air of rooms
Through which journeys in cool motionlessness a god of ash

He tires an orchard of iron-pieces /
Betrayed / soon saved by the brother bird
Shedding at the peak of its leap its brilliant wings

A bride is in an empty shadow
Her water breasts are long night dust
Her fingers shielded by autumnal beings

*

Traversed and pure, houses
Of brittle ancientness / those
Passed through of cold thresholds, their
Faces of gleaming dust

Then withdrawn into the
Blind solitude of pollen-bursting splendour. The
Body of several young nights, lightened by
Voided clusters of fruit –

Then goat-like eternalness
Will graze the minimum. Daylight. The bosom
Will go forth / burning.

*

Contre neige ! La rose assouvit un losange
Céleste. Un oiseau traverse le bosquet
D'achèvement tracé par le nuage rare

Sous le couteau du vent / lampe profonde et pure
Arrête, aux environs de plusieurs lignes froides,
Ce peuple absent réfléchi dans la rivière

La vérité d'ici : ce sel
Aux mains de l'éternelle assise méditante,
L'ombre du vieux soleil avec sa chèvre noire

*

Et l'astre nu du vent s'épuise ! Son miroir
Endormi dans le corps entier de la lumière
Vérifiera l'épouse identique, et le sable

La cruche avant l'épaule
Sera restituée aux anges des labours,
Disposée dans le vide et de défaite vive

Oblique, le sein pauvre
Ma grande sombre mère entourée de vieux arbres
Regarde un feu tenir les arbres, puis son bras

*

Against snow! The rose satiates a celestial
Rhomb. A bird flies through the grove
Of completion traced out by the rare cloud

Under the wind's knife / deep and pure lamp
Halts, around several cold lines,
This absent people reflected in the river

The truth of here : this salt
In the hands of eternal woman sitting in meditation,
The shadow of the old sun with its black goat

*

And the wind's naked star fades exhausted! Its mirror
Asleep in the full body of light
Will confirm the identical spouse, and the sand

The pitcher before the shoulder
Will be restored to the angels of the tilled land,
Set out in the void and of sparkling defeat

Oblique, the poor bosom
My great dark mother surrounded by old trees
Watches a fire hold the trees, and then her arm

*

de **L'être poupée** (1983)

Colombe incendiant la formation
Des larmes dans leur trahison limpide
Enjolivant le bélier du paysage
Celui par qui le temps est conservé
Sous la flamme à peine formée des liserons
La brume est au centre du centre : cela
Brille, et l'arbre au centre de l'arbre
Il donne un peu de son nom à ceux qui pensent
Et les retient par serment de transparence

*

Le blé est le fils de cela dans la lumière
Impliquée dans la joliesse et trace
Avant le sable de gravure, la racine
Inouïe de l'explosion : arbre d'orage
Le pied brûlé par inversion métaphysique
Au ciel affiné de colombes, larmes larmes
Devoir du cœur en la beauté pensive
De sarcophage ici que rompt l'arbre

*

Rivage, l'arbre et l'emmêlement des rives
Dans le désordre de l'orage au matin
À cause d'une idée ô dévêtue
Avivant l'être en son théâtre inapparent
L'image s'étant retirée, la parole
Livre son blé à des oiseaux limpides
Volant l'aurore aux gardiens des eaux vives
Avant de s'effacer dans l'écriture

*

from **Doll Being** (1983)

Dove setting afire the creation
Of tears in their limpid betrayal
Prettifying the landscape's ram
By whom time is conserved
Beneath the barely formed flame of wild convolvulus
Mist is at the centre of the centre : all
Is brilliant, and the tree at the tree's centre
Gives something of its name to those in thought
And holds them back through oath of transparency

*

The wheat is the son of that in the light
Insinuated in prettiness and traces
Before the engraving sand, the incredible
Root of the explosion : storm tree
The base burned by metaphysical inversion
In the sky refined with doves, tears tears
Heart's duty within the pensive sarcophagal
Beauty here that the tree ruptures

*

Shore, the tree and the tanglement of embankments
In the disorder of the morning storm
Because of an idea oh she that is unclothed
Exciting being in its unapparent theatre
Image having withdrawn, speech
Delivers its wheat to limpid birds
Stealing dawn from the keepers of running waters
Before erasure in writing

*

Surgie avec les insectes diurnes
Comme herbe notre enfance aux yeux humides
Terre de brume éparpillée et terre
Où se façonne une mémoire d'herbe
Autour des lampes désœuvrées et tout le givre
Garde profonde une lueur d'épée
De qui s'est retiré le bruit du fer
Afin de remembrer le vent dans l'arbre

*

Et qui de jour énoncera le blé
Fermé sur l'autre blé de transparence
Tous les oiseaux formés et tous les cercles
Qui se défont et se refont ensemble
Interrompant le chant aveugle : chaise
Abandonnée sur un balcon rompu
Par des amants plus affinés que cendre
Aux équations arides, leur ortie ?

*

Sur elle est l'à peine brillant croissant de gel
Surgi très seul de la matière avec ses loups
Tenant tribune de parole aux limpides
Araignées ivres de leur soie constellée
Et le poète est allongé dans l'écriture
Dans une chambre en une chambre tenue
Son beau prénom bleu par immanence
Aux fins mathématiques de la lune

*

Surging forth with diurnal insects
Like grass our childhood with its wet eyes
Earth of scattered mist and earth
Where is fashioned a memory of grass
Around lamps fallen idle and such frost
Shields deep a sword's glinting
From which the noise of iron has withdrawn
So as to give limbs once more to the wind in the tree

*

And who of a day will state the wheat
Closed upon the other wheat of transparency
All the birds formed and all the circles
That are unmade and remade together
Interrupting the blind song : a chair
Deserted on a broken balcony
By lovers more refined than ash
With its arid equations, their stinging nettle ?

*

Upon her is the barely shining crescent of frost
Risen most solitary from matter with its wolves
Holding tribune of speech before the limpid
Spiders drunk on their constellated silk
And the poet stretched out in writing
In a room within a room held
His fine name turned blue out of inherence
In the mathematical ends of the moon

*

Tout l'arbre de l'esprit dans le visible
Et le voilier de tout son être brûle
Si déliée douleur de la substance
Gardant voilier à l'embouchure de ses lignes
Si déliée douleur de la disante
Comme une veuve arrimée dans la parole
Et chaque cil est un enfant en pleurs
Avec les anges de la nuit sur la substance

*

Et tous les bois sont des bois d'agonie
Selon une beauté d'intellection
En qui s'enferme un lion spirituel
Idée seconde en qui l'harmonie flambe
Et flambe aussi de ses genoux limpides
L'enfant voilé de feu par abstraction
S'il est le fils il est voilé d'un monde
Où brûle l'épée noire des moissons

*

Or toute nuit étant algèbre pure
Aux marges de cela qui fut écrit
Dans le flamboiement du reflet du feu du nom
Brûlant dans le sommeil de l'innommé
Sous l'astre ou arbre des stérilités diurnes
La fille donc fermera ses bras réels
Sur l'aigle sombre de l'esprit ayant blanchi
D'être nocturne et miroir d'oliveraies

*

The whole tree of the mind in the visible
And the sailing vessel of its entire being is burning
Such unbound pain of substance
Shielding sailing vessel at the mouth of its lines
Such unbound pain of her who says
Like a widow moored to speech
And each eyelash is a child in tears
With the angels of night upon substance

*

And all woods are woods of dying
According to a beauty of intellection
Within which is locked a spiritual lion
Second idea within which harmony flares
And blazes too from its limpid knees
The child veiled in fire through abstraction
If he is the son he is veiled with a world
Wherein burns the black sword of harvests

*

Now every night being pure algebra
In the margins of that which was written
In the blazing of the reflection from the fire of the name
Burning in the sleep of the unnamed
Beneath the star or tree of diurnal barrennesses
The daughter then will fold her real arms
Upon the dark eagle of the mind whitened
From being nocturnal and mirror of olive groves

*

Et face à l'aube en qui un fer exerce
Une forme irradiant le sens
Un autre feu formé de tous les signes
Rompt le nuage enraciné dans l'œuvre
: Ce sont nuées de noir velours, âmes voilées
Voilant le sens en langues d'incendie
Par médiation du lion spirituel
Aux fixités du torrent donnant sa face

*

Père irrêvé dans la violence du non-être
Buvant à une ombre de cruche une eau de rêve
Qui se mélange à ce qui fut, bouche éblouie
Par le soleil irréversible du sein,
Terrible cerf cassant ses branches contre l'esprit
Et qui s'en va nûment : ses branches tremblent
Dans l'eau ardente de la femme aux braises lentes
Tandis que tournent sous le vent le fleuve et l'arc

*

Colombe non physique ornant le fer
Avec la foule des colombes désœuvrées
Son ventre est une lampe en bleu futur
Inouïe larme elle est enfance en Dieu
Et toute l'herbe de son ventre la rattache
À la lumière du grand fleuve au corps de braise
Pris dans le feu intérieur de son armure
Jusqu'aux méandres de la mer chargée de perles

*

And in the face of dawn wherein an iron tool effects
A form radiating meaning
Another fire made up of all signs
Breaks open the cloud rooted in the work
: Clouds that are of black velvet, veiled souls
Veiling meaning in tongues of fire
By mediation of the spiritual lion
Giving to the torrent's fixities its face

*

Undreamed father in the violence of no-being
Drinking from a pitcher's shadow a dreamed water
That mingles with what was, mouth dazzled
By the irreversible sun of the bosom,
Terrible stag breaking its antlers against the spirit
And moving off in nakedness : its antlers tremble
In the ardent water of slow-embered woman
While beneath the wind spin and turn the river and the bow

*

Non-physical dove decorating the ironwork
With the throng of idle doves
Her womb is a lamp of future blueness
Unparalleled tear she is childhood in God
And all the grass of her womb ties her
To the light of the great river of embered body
Caught in the inner fire of its armour
And the very meanderings of the sea weighed down with pearls

*

Comme violon conduit à son bois pur
Quand la splendeur de l'être se retourne
Pour une lune de poussière et de feuillage
Ornementée du luxe de la mort,
Est la parole. Elle donne un peu de braise
Au fils qui lui naquit blé noir du monde :
(De quel soleil son évangile, en quelle langue?)
– Biches de l'herbe, aimez mon cœur

*

Une colombe gémit, elle est impure
Et supposée (une colombe?) miroitante
Comme poupée de tragédie : éclat ou arc
Brisé dans l'herbe irréservée Ici respire
Au centre de la gravité du centre
Près de la lampe une enfance cristalline
Elle est matière de la flèche elle est brisée
: Lumière en éclat de lumière en éclat...

*

Et la poupée de cendre et d'air natal
Comme une perle entre des cils de mer...
Elle attend l'absolu de l'air, ayant des arcs;
Elle pense à la netteté du nuage.
Peut-être s'en va-t-elle une fois aux méandres
Du fleuve. Qui est l'esprit. Qu'elle est. Mystère
De la poupée... Le vent qui la connut
La refait un peu, puis s'effraie

*

Like a violin brought to its pure wood
When the splendour of being turns about
For a moon of dust and foliage
Ornamented with the luxury of death,
Is speech. It gives of its embers
To the son born to it black wheat of the world :
(Of what sun its gospel, in what language ?)
– Does of the grass, bring love to my heart

*

A dove moans, it is impure
And deemed (a dove ?) shimmering
Like a doll of tragedy : glittering splinter or bow
Broken in the unreserved grass Here breathes
At the centre of gravity's centre
By the lamp a crystalline childhood
It is matter of arrow it is broken
: Light as splintered light as glittering splinter...

*

And the doll of ash and native air
Like a pearl between ocean eyelashes...
She awaits the absoluteness of air, possessing bows;
She thinks of the sharp clarity of cloud.
Perhaps she once moves off toward the meanderings
Of the river. Which is spirit. Which she is. Strange mystery
Of the doll... The wind that knew her
Refashions her briefly, then catches fright

*

Et le poète ! Il la dit la poésie
Vitreuse et par projection de figure
Selon son corps et sur son corps qui se dévêt
Sous la montée désordonnée des astres
Dans un espace : elle joue à la marelle
Avec elle-même en songe de l'esprit
: En lui elle est pauvre poupée mortelle
: Il est en elle l'enfant de ses genoux

*

Un pas se fit. Dans l'herbe. Et c'est un peu
La lune dans la symétrie mirante
Qui se défait avec cérémonie
Autour de rien, herbeusement dans l'herbe :
« Herbeusement dans l'extinction de l'herbe ».
Un autre pas se fit : chemin d'aveugle
Barque empierrée en disparition de pierres
Avant l'éclipse au surgissement des chiens

*

Dieu de la nuit de l'être dans le songe
Sous tant de larmes avec des larmes, l'arbre
Comme le chant du rossignol dévêt
Les feuilles de la mer et tous les fleuves
Question brillante aux cils de la plus nue
Son sein salé absent de la substance
Et la voici question ou longue lampe
Exagérée par l'absolu de l'air

*

And the poet! He calls her poetry
Of glass and by figured projection
According to her body and upon her body unclothed
Beneath the disordered rise of stars
In a space : she plays hopscotch
By herself in a daydream of the mind
: Within him she is poor mortal doll
: He is within her the child of her knees

*

A step was taken. In the grass. And it is like
The moon in mirroring symmetry
That is unmade ceremoniously
Around nothing, grassily in the grass :
'Grassily in the extinction of the grass.'
Another step was taken : blind man's path
A boat paved over like stones disappearing
Before the eclipse as dogs surge forth

*

God of the night of being in daydream
Beneath so many tears with tears, the tree
Like the nightingale's song unrobes
The leaves of the sea and all rivers
Shining question upon the eyelashes of the most naked
Her salty bosom absent from substance
And here she is like a question or long lamp
Grown vast through the absoluteness of the air

*

Ma lumineuse ma liée mon adorante
Dans tes rectangles nuageux une bougie
Par forme et par façon de nuit tremblante
Voilant ton nom d'embrasement nocturne
Et tout le sang qui fait briller ton corps en blé
Comme une neige endormie dans la neige
Au carrefour de toute lampe divisée
Non frontalière de l'esprit et des fragments

*

Dieu de la nuit de l'être dans l'esprit
Accorde ta rosée à une enfance
Évanouie par aube, ramifiée
En beauté pauvre de ceci : une fillette
Comme au mystère de ses jambes la parure
D'un peu de sang   Et le cri est dans l'ange
Un arbre vert, et vert, déployé
Sur la fillette ensommeillée d'orties

*

Et toute cruche est idée suspendue
Avant sa forme de poussière, dans l'attente
D'une colombe de silence aux pieds de pluie
Colombe fiancée aux invisibles
Et c'est théâtre ici de forme vide
Comme une fille d'harmonie et qui attend
D'être comblée : une mesure l'emplit;
– Gazelle vaine, elle est source tremblante

*

My luminous my bound my adoring one
In your cloudy rectangles a candle
Through form and nocturnal fashion trembling
Veiling your name in night's blaze
And all the blood that makes your wheated body shine forth
Like snow asleep in snow
At the crossroads of every riven lamp
Not fronting upon mind and upon fragments

*

God of the night of being in our spirits
Grant your dew to a childhood
Vanished through dawn, branching out
In this poor beauty : a young girl
Like in the mystery of her legs the adornment
Of blood trickling   And the angel cries out
A green, and green, tree, spread forth
Upon the girl in the nettles of sleep

*

And every pitcher is idea suspended
Before its dusty form, in expectancy
Of a dove of rain-footed silence
A dove betrothed to those invisible
And here is theatre of empty form
Like a daughter of harmony awaiting
Fulfilment : a measuredness enters her entire;
– Vain gazelle, she is quivering source

*

Et l'Être avec bonté se retourne
– Et nous regarde mourir. Les violettes
De ses mains tremblent d'un éclat incomparable
Au labyrinthe de ses ongles de rosée.
Miroir des lèvres de ciguë ! elles s'éteignent,
Et les poupées terribles dans les rues.
L'amour défait ses vieux cheveux. L'Être tremble.
Une étoile de pluie rompt l'horizon.

*

And Being with kindness turns about
– And gazes on our dying. The violets
Of its hands shake with incomparable splendour
In the labyrinth of its bedewed fingernails.
Mirror of hemlock lips! Their light fades away,
And the terrible dolls in the streets.
Love lets down its old hair. Being trembles.
A star of rain breaks open the horizon.

*

de Fragments : Poème (1978)

Si
L'esprit contre l'esprit
Se dresse
Qui sauvera de son épée l'esprit ?

Visages dehors / dans la géométrie
Froide. L'épée
Et son chemin
Sont conversion de l'herbe

. S'allonge une épée dure au sein noir.
La main que double
Une rosée
De feu, de faim

*

Le corps n'est plus le corps. Il est
Formé de pauvre ciel au bout des rues
Que traverse le peigne du matin. Il est
L'ami de la femme nocturne avec ses jambes

Ô douleur de ses jambes ! ô sur moi
Que vient mal respirer le chien visible
Ce mélange de moi et d'elle et nous
Désireux d'être respirés émerveillants

Qui de nos corps aura faim et soif très tard
Quand sera la question terrible
Sur nous penchée avec son visage irradiant
À l'envers de la nuit et du jour, tremblante ?

*

from Fragments: Poem (1978)

If
Spirit against spirit
Rises up
Who with his sword will save spirit

Faces outside / in the cold
Geometry. The sword
And its path
Are conversion of the grass

. Stretches forth a sword hard upon the black bosom.
The hand doubled
By a dew
Of fire, of hunger

*

The body is no longer body. It is
Shaped by meagre sky at the end of streets
That morning's comb runs through. It is
The friend of nocturnal woman with her legs

Oh aching of her legs! Oh upon me
The visible dog sniffs clumsily away
This mixture of me and her and both
Desirous of being breathed in in wonder

Who will hunger and thirst late late after our bodies
When will the terrible question be
Stooped over us with its irradiant face
On the far side of night and day, trembling away?

*

Pure figure (dents aussi) d'antique
Rouge :
Menaçant la face du feu. Quand
Vont les jambes de dense soierie
Nocturne, en pierre d'hier, jambes.

Doutant. Une prairie, tremblant. Elles
Tranchent le feu de la figure faible
Sur le lit fleuri de toujours. Puis,
Confient le jour au matin exigu.

Figures pour figures, jouent
À qui le jeu. Le disparu voisin
Écoute un feu se faire :
négation.

*

Quand sera la question terrible
Sur nous penchée avec son visage irradiant
Le doigt désignera l'autre brûlé visage
Se regardant

Désignera la direction de non-
direction / de non-visage avec
Le miroir de non-miroir avec
La main cherchant le double désignant

Sera le doigt de désignation nulle
Parmi les objets du miroir, le nom
Enfui / observant
Mourir ou prendre corps l'autre question

*

Pure figure (teeth too) of ancient
Red :
Threatening the face of fire. When
Move forth legs of silken night density,
Like yesterday's stone, legs.

Doubting. A meadow, trembling. They
Slice through the fire of the faint figure
Upon the ever-flowered bed. Then,
Entrust the day to the scant morning.

Figures for figures, playing
Whose turn to play. The lost neighbour
Listens to a fire taking :
negation.

*

When the terrible question is
Stooped over us with its irradiant face
The finger will designate the other burnt face
Gazing upon itself

Will designate the direction of no-
direction / of no-face with
The mirror of no-mirror with
The hand seeking the image designating

Will be the finger of null designation
Amongst the mirror's objects, the vanished
/ observing name
To die or to incarnate the other question

*

L'absurde corps désirant
Est dans l'éclat de pierre, lit sans feuilles
L'angle du soir le blessant

Beau corps d'avant l'été, dis
La pierre froide, la pierre éclairant
; l'oiseau recouvrant.

Le blé n'étant, le corps a faim
Du pain d'avant la femme. De /
Quel blé – ou quel nom ?

*

Sera l'amour dans le miroir du fils

Mère éclaircie dans la seconde chambre
L'esprit ombré par l'acuité du fil
Brisant le fil, la double double main
Dans le froid lumineux de l'autre chambre

Dressant l'absence en dure adoration
De qui ? Jambes de qui ? Brûlant l'esprit
Du fils formé dans le feu du miroir
L'esprit ayant dénaturé sa hanche

Sera l'amour, puis la blessure, ornant
L'image. Puis sera
La fête avec la densité des jambes
Massacrées. Sera le massacre par le fils.

*

The absurd body of desire
Is in the slivered flash of stone, the leafless bed
The angle of evening cutting into it

Lovely body from before summer, speak
The cold stone, stone illuminating
; the bird recovering.

Wheat not being, the body hungers
For the bread from before woman. For /
What wheat – or what name?

*

Will be love in the mirror of the son

Mother clarified in the second room
The mind shadowed by the sharpness of thread
Breaking thread, the double double hand
In the luminous cold of the other room

Raising up absence as hard adoration
Of whom? Legs of whom? Burning the mind
Of the son formed in the mirror's fire
Mind having denatured its hip

Will be love, then wound, decorating
Image. Then will be
Celebration with the denseness of legs
Slaughtered. Will be slaughter by the son.

*

Il va tomber dans les volutes de l'empire
Et disparaître en des langues d'abstraction
Laissant de beaux morceaux de monde ou songe
Aux peurs aux enfantines

Invité des versets
Sur ce versant avec l'incendie des aspects
Les deux mains sans
L'autre désir brûlant l'interne jambe

Il connaîtra Montagne
Nocturne bourdonnante du vol des ours
Ô Nathalie
La larme de son sexe
Coulant dans la bouche orageuse et bue par l'interdite

*

Ô fils ! criant incorporé dans l'arbre
Protégeant le milieu du souffle, soufflant
L'obscure lampe

Et toute terre étant voisine, allant
Vers la non-poésie de terre, tenant
Le fruit de souffle obscur

Non-poésie de terre criant
Poésie de non-poésie criant
Que terre soit le précieux deuil

*

He will fall into the whorls of empire
And disappear in languages of abstraction
Leaving behind fine bits of world or daydream
In fears in infant classes

The guest of verses
Upon this versant in the inferno of appearances
Both hands without
The other desire burning the internal leg

He will know Mountain
Of night humming from the flight of bears
Oh Nathalie
The tear of her sex
Flowing into the stormy mouth and drunk down by her who is
                                                    forbidden

*

Oh son! crying out integrated with tree
Guarding the midst of breath, blowing upon
The obscure lamp

And every earth being adjacent, moving
Towards the no-poetry of earth, holding
The fruit of obscure breath

No-poetry of earth crying out
Poetry of no-poetry crying out
That earth may be the precious sorrowing

*

La pensée sera consumée et ses ongles
Puis recueillie dans une image nulle
Les ongles demeurant dans la maison limpide

Double maison dans le céleste ciel
Avec l'autre maison approfondie de brume
Puis l'eau mirant la brume sans maison

Double simple maison dans les racines
Du ciel inhabité, pensée pure
Cherchant, d'impure brume, la ressemblance

*

Le cœur est nu et le talon meurtri,
De la déesse. Elle observe la chasse.
Limpide rouge est le beau saignement
Consolidant la pierre

L'absolue tête en d'absolus branchages
Regarde en elle une éternité d'eau
Éveiller la pensée vieillie du lac :
Brillant, brillant, nacre ou mémoire ?

Et quelle chasse ? La déesse
Retient le sang du plus profond arbuste
Avant de confier à son être lumineux
La fleur fermée de l'être

*

Thought will be consumed and its claws
Then gathered in a null image
Its claws dwelling on in the limpid house

Doubled house within the celestial sky
With the other house deepened with mist
Then water mirroring the houseless mist

Double single house amongst the roots
Of uninhabited sky, pure thought
Seeking, of impure mist, resemblance

*

The heart is naked and the talon bruised,
Of the goddess. She gazes on the hunt.
Limpid red is the beautiful bleeding
Strengthening stone

The absolute head in absolute boughs
Watches within itself an eternity of water
Awakening the aged thought of the lake :
Shimmering, brilliant, mother of pearl or memory ?

And what hunt ? The goddess
Holds back the blood of the deepest shrub
Before entrusting to its luminous being
The closed flower of being

*

Brûlure en ce non-miroir de non-brûlure
De la plus pauvre en sa liante image
Non rosie en un corps d'antiques jambes
Ayant l'identité de vieillie cendre

L'épée l'ayant tranchée pour le don
D'une corbeille en don d'incandescence
Sa jambe étant vivante et rattachée
À l'obscur muet remuement d'une jambe

Funèbre et non funèbre éclat de lignes
Réunies dans une beauté de siècle d'arbre
L'herbe étant justifiée en quatre membres
De non-visage, retenant l'obscure image

*

Araignée de la parole, absence
D'insecte dans l'immensité neigeuse
Sans arbre à creuser-dominer la parole

Araignée de mille araignées de mille
Nuages compliqués de mille
Négations; puis l'arbre, ô jet pur

De puits sculpté. L'araignée
Profonde complice d'eau profonde
– Ici la neige étant neige et premier puits

*

Burning within this no-mirror of no-burning
Of the poorest woman in her binding image
Not carnadine in a body of ancient legs
Having the identity of aged ash

The sword having sliced through her for the gift
Of a basket like a gift of incandescence
Her leg being alive and linked
To the obscure mute stirring of a leg

Funereal and unfunereal splintering of lines
Gathered into a beauty of century of tree
Grass being justified as four limbs
Of no-face, retaining the obscure image

*

Spider of speech, absence
Of insect in the snowy vastness
With no tree deepening-dominating speech

Spider of a thousand spiders of a thousand
Tangled clouds of a thousand
Negations; then the tree, oh pure spurting

Of sculpted wellspring. The spider
Deep accomplice of deep water
– Here snow being snow and first wellspring

*

Contre le pur, contre cela : impur
Sarcophage avec ses racines –
Et l'arbre dans le nom de l'arbre désirant
La fin du nom et le début de l'arbre

La terre autour obscure – contre
Cela : le beau sein noir par désir
De terre obscure, lui brillant
D'enfance, tombeau proche

Le sein interrogeant l'écrit de l'arbre
Sur la lumière entrant dans le sarcophage
Ouvert aux anges de la respiration
Fiévreux dans les images

*

Parole, et l'arbre contenu. Parole
Avec l'arbre des mots dans le corps d'arbre
Et le corps féminin des mots
Dans la droiture inexpliquée de l'arbre

Tous liquides miroirs criants de vent
Puis retenus dans l'anxiété des racines
Sous le nom de la terre qui est
Corps de terre imagée dans l'arbre

Corps féminin de terre avec les bras
Formant l'arbre, et de femme
Ô miroir ô souffrant
Pour l'étendue de terre défaite et ses liaisons

*

Against the pure, against that : impure
Sarcophagus with its roots –
And tree in the name of tree desiring
The end of naming and beginning of tree

The earth all around dark – against
That : the lovely black bosom out of desire
For obscure earth, brilliant
With childhood, tomb close by

The bosom questioning the written text of tree
Upon the light entering the sarcophagus
Open to the angels of breathing
Fevered in images

*

Speech, and tree contained. Speech
With the tree of words in the body of tree
And the feminine body of words
In the unexplained uprightness of the tree

All liquid mirrors screaming with wind
Then held back in the anxiety of roots
Beneath the name of the earth that is
Body of earth imaged in tree

Feminine body of earth with arms
Shaping tree, and of woman
Oh mirror oh suffering
For the expanse of undone earth and its ligatures

*

Restitution d'antique épouse. Loi
Du pied avec le sol.
En l'unifiée fermée : d'herbe, ou fautive ?

Et front léger avec le sein de celle.

Si mourir d'être, ô bouche à non-mourir
De mort factice, et bouche de mourir

Sa bouche est certifiée dans l'herbe. Restitu-
tion d'antique, et presque, idée de sein. Le
Nuage est doux et creux, et doux, sur le sein

*

Nuage enraciné dans la parole
En ce jardin de saisie nulle
Criant son cri d'autre beauté, criant

En ce visage. L'instant d'une verdure
Sur ce visage. Ô
Arbre en saisie d'arbre.

Incorruptiblement dans la parole.
Ô arbre
En ce jardin.
Niant le don impur de ce visage
Incorruptible, fiancé, pauvreté.

*

Restoring of ancient spouse. Law
Of foot with ground.
Within her closed, unified : of grass, or at fault?

And light temple and the bosom of her.
If dying from being, oh mouth of no-dying
Of factitious death, and mouth of dying

Her mouth is attested in grass. Rest-
oration of ancientness and, almost, idea of bosom. The
Cloud is soft and hollow, and soft, upon her bosom

*

Cloud rooted in speech
Within this garden of null seizure
Crying out its cry of other beauty, crying out

Within this face. The moment of a greenness
Upon this face. Oh
Tree like a seizure of tree.

Incorruptibly in speech.
Oh tree
Within this garden.
Denying the impure gift of this face
Incorruptible, betrothed, poverty.

*

Le dénuement : ceci :
Sur nous la marque de mourir, dessinée
Et dans l'idée une fourrure avec le soir

Et dans l'esprit la grappe en la douleur
Découronnée, son bleu et pur friable
Étant brûlant visage

Poussière aimant poussière aimant poussière
L'épée criant d'une broussaille par l'oiseau
Cassant les directions

*

De non-mourir étant mourir, dé si clair.
Bourgeon parleur dans la joliesse
Têtue. Parlant nuage.

Mais la parole ayant parlé. Qui
Donc de jolie bouche est dure joliesse ?
Mourir étant parmi joli mourir

Dans l'explosion : et ce désordre de paroles
Avec les fruits, le long soudain silence
: Puis le passant défini par ce silence

*

Destitution : this :
Upon us the mark of dying, drawn
And in the mind a furring in the night

And in the head the cluster of fruit within pain
Uncrowned, its blue and pure brittleness
Being burning face

Dust loving dust loving dust
The sword crying out from the underwood via the bird
Shattering directions

*

Of no-dying being dying, such transparent dice.
Glib bud in the stubborn
Prettiness. Speaking cloud.

But speech having spoken. Who
Then of pretty mouth is hard prettiness?
Dying being amongst pretty dying

In the explosion : and this disorder of words
Spoken with fruit, the long sudden silence
: Then the passer-by defined by this silence

*

Vers la fin de l'amour
Étoile entrebaîllée l'amande
Ainsi brillant,

Par l'huile enracinée.
(La Purifiée dans la lumière
: contenue)

Retombée la violente mesure d'arbres
– Toute lumière enfin restituée
Pour rejoindre, se déroutant, le froid.

*

Tombeau en la parole étroite
D'étroite mère et de nul fils
Que l'arbre enraciné dans l'inscription
Furtive, d'une terre

Le long de l'être en sa coutume, le cristallin
(Vivant) respire, et le ciel retenu
Respire au pierreux crépuscule, pierre envolée…

Pardons ravis sur ce balcon de tombe :
La jeune et jeune mère
Veille endormie, amour étincelant

*

Towards the end of love
Half-open star its kernel
Thus gleaming,

From the rooted oil.
(She Purified in the light
         : contained)

Subsided the violent measure of trees
– All light at last restored
To join once more, adrift, the cold.

*

Tomb within close speech
Of close mother and no son
But the tree rooted in furtive
Inscription, of some earth

Alongside being within its custom, (living)
Crystallinity breathes, and the sky held back
Breathes in the stony dusk, like a stone on the wing...

Forgivings snatched upon this tomb-like balcony :
The young and young mother
Watches in her sleep, love sparkling

*

Dame de faim aux carreaux attachée
Adressée au brouillard des ronces
Dans l'abstraction de tes jolies voix nues

Et le poète en poésie, voici
Son orteil dur par le sablier d'herbe
Son doigt de transparence désignant

Le fruit du pain mortel sous le sommeil
Ardent et triste et rayonnant, la faim,
Dame de faim, enterrée la balance
Et fermée la mesure

*

Le blé, il saignera avec le millénaire
Venu d'hier, ange illettré, sa main
Brillant, éternité, froid dormeur

Et froide enfance, robe, éternité si froide
À plis et blés subtils tuée la terre
Exaspérant, mirée, la mendiante

Main pure en exaspération d'aumône :
Ni pure ou pire ici, l'ange dormeur
Aimant, cruel, ses cruautés premières

*

Lady of hunger clinging to the panes
Turned to the fog of brambles
In the abstractness of your lovely naked voices

And the poet in poetry, here
Is his hard toe via the grassy hour-glass
His finger of transparency designating

The fruit of mortal bread beneath sleep
Ardent and sad and radiant, hunger,
Lady of hunger, her scales buried deep
And her measures closed

*

Wheat, wheat will bleed with the millennium
Arisen from yesterday, illiterate angel, its hand
Gleaming, eternity, cold slumberer

And cold childhood, robe, eternity of such coldness
Of subtle folds and wheats the earth slain
Exasperating, mirrored, she who begs

Pure hand out of exasperated charity :
Neither pure or worse, here, the slumbering angel
Loving, cruel, its prime cruelties

*

Sans fleurs est la maison limpide
D'Isis brillant en la froideur du sein

Le fruit s'est retiré. L'arbre est principe.

Épée du froid dans le principe, ombre
D'iris cruels par ce feu dur, ô soie
Embarrassant, fumée, l'ombre envolée

*

La non-touchée, terre, ô inenterrée
Aucunement, en la forêt-principe :
Son fruit formé, fraîcheur inaltérée

Inétendue. Et sol d'œillet tragique !
Courue la terre, en arbres, non courue
Lampe cherchant, de terre, aveugles cils.

De terre et d'autre, ô sœur inenterrée
Gardienne en soi de l'œil en son principe
Par ce noir soir, terre et fruit, irradiant

*

Without flowers is the limpid house
Of Isis gleaming with the coldness of the bosom

The fruit has withdrawn. The tree is principle.

Sword of coldness in the principle, shadow
Of cruel irises by this hard fire, oh silk
Encumbering, like smoke, the shadow in flight

*

She the untouched, earth, oh unburied
Utterly, within the forest-principle :
Her fruit formed, coolness unaltered

Unextended. And soil of tragical carnation !
The earth roamed, like trees, unroamed
Lamp seeking, earth-like, unseeing lashes.

Of earth and otherness, oh unburied sister
Guardian within of the eye within its principle
On this black evening, earth and fruit, radiating

*

Arbre inversé dans le nuage
Ou disparu nocturne
La forme enfin brisée l'huile envolée

Ô lampe   d'une   lampe
Noueuse enracinée
Dans une terre étroite et nulle avec
L'incendie des aspects

(Où seul, de jeune mère, brilla le sein)

Ô nuit de nuit formée ô nuageuse
– Dans l'inversion   :

«Nous veillerons en compagnie de la parole»

Sans cri, à portée d'arc   :

*

Tree inverted in cloud
Or disappeared nocturnal
Form at last broken the oil taken to flight

Oh lamp   of a   lamp
Knotty rooted
In an earth narrow and null with
The inferno of appearances

(Where alone, young mother's, shone bright the bosom)

Oh night of night formed oh clouded one
– In inversion   :

'We shall keep watch in the company of speech'

Never crying out, bow within reach   :

*

de Obscure lampe de cela (1979)

Mon arc ou ma brûlure
Portés en ce miroir ailleurs qu'en lui
La forme de ma forme en destruction
De vive lampe vive

Lampe d'acanthe
Nuage est dans une âme en forme de
Nuage en forme de
Brûlant nuage

Arc :
– Contre la nuit formée de ces nuages
Son visage éclairé du peu terrestre
Froid
      , de ce nuage.

*

: de ceci, lampe nouée amoureusement
L'huile d'une parole proférée
La nuit tombée sur une lampe, la
Langue en cette lampe a racine

Le froid muettement
D'avant (après) le nœud des lampes, flamme
En cette lampe par ces nœuds déliée

Et qui parlera, lampe, mal-
– Gré le souffle qui sur   elle   soufflera
Langue parlant de lampe
La femme assise à l'écouter obscure
Tenant sur ses genoux genoux
                ses mains obscures

*

from Obscure Lamp of That (1979)

My bow or my burning
Borne up within this mirror yet not in it
The form of my form like a destruction
Of live living lamp

Acanthus lamp
Cloud is in a soul in the shape of
Cloud in the shape of
Burning cloud

Bow :
– Against the night shaped from these clouds
Its face lit up by the barely earthly
Cold
    , of this cloud.

*

: of this, a lamp lovingly knotted
The oil of uttered speech
Night fallen upon a lamp, language
Within this lamp finds root

The cold beyond speech
Before (after) the knot of lamps, a flame
Within this lamp by these knots unbound

And who will speak, lamp, des-
– Pite the breath that upon   it   will breathe
Language speaking of lamp
Woman sitting listening to it in obscurity
Holding upon her knees knees
                    her obscure hands

*

Idée en elle, obscure.
Fermée (idée fermée) sur une lampe

À peine, et de peu, allumée. Portée
De froid en froid jusqu'en
L'état obscur, aggravée, près du sang.

*

Retirée en pensée obscure
Est lampe obscure
En elle est la pensée
De (presque) lampe en sa lampe retirée
Afin de conserver

L'obscure lampe de cela, lampe de gel
/ Cela s'étant produit par neige
Cernant la neige et la lampe, et cela

*

Lampe de gel fruitée de neige
Le jour parmi le jour c'est lumière
Entre les mains de qui fera le jour

Pour une lampe endormie puis éveillée
En une seconde lampe éclaboussée
De froid mais éveillée par l'éveil

Tombe
De la parole
                    : recueillie pour la cendre

*

Idea within her, obscure.
Closed (idea closed) upon a lamp

Barely lit, and from so little. Borne
From cold to cold to within
The darkened state, worsened, close to blood.

*

Withdrawn into obscure thought
Is obscure lamp
Within her is the thought
Of (nearly) lamp withdrawn within her lamp
So as to keep alive

The obscure lamp of that, lamp of frozenness
/ That having come about through snow
Hemming in snow and lamp, and that

*

Lamp of frozenness snow-fruited
Daylight amidst daylight is light
In the hands of whoever will make day

For a lamp asleep then awakened
Within a second lamp splashed
With cold but awakened by waking

Tomb
Of speech
          : gathered for its ash

*

Oliveraie définie par la neige
Attachée à ce peu
:　　　aube arrachée aux racines

Comme arbre d'aucune sorte de qui
S'est approchée l'approche
En compagnie d'aucune nuit

– Dénonçant par l'olivier le peu
Et formulant la perfection neigeuse
En profondeur absoute

*

De neige – d'incertitude
Formée forgée par un marteau fatal
En nœud, presque, de froid

… Que rature une étoile enrésillée
(Advenue à la déchirure de la lampe
Pour sauver la lumière　　　:)

Au-dessus du champ brillant de neige
Où va la neige avec
Ceci brisant cela

*

Lampe la joue dévorée par les arbres
En ce jardin de terre, celui-là
Consolidant le feu

Non-feu se repliant dans une lampe
Dite et redite, soudain proférée
Et posée là sur la table du jour

Attendant, table, le bois et les liaisons
De l'être à demi fidèle à l'arbre
Au feu à demi, par la lampe endeuillé

*

Olive grove defined by snow
Tied to this minimum
:   dawn torn from its roots

Like a tree of no kind that
Has been approached by approach itself
In the company of no night

– Denouncing through the olive tree this minimum
And formulating snowy perfection
As depth absolved

*

From snow – from uncertainty
Shaped forged by a fatal hammer
Like a knot, almost, of coldness

… That a reticulate star erases
(Fallen to the rending of the lamp
To save the light   :)

Above the field shining bright with snow
Where snow goes forth with
This breaking apart that

*

Lamp the cheek devoured by trees
Within this garden of earth, itself
Strengthening the fire

No-fire folding back within a lamp
Spoken and spoken again, suddenly uttered
And placed there upon the table of day

Table awaiting the wood and the linkages
Of being, half-faithful to the tree
Half to the fire, cast into mourning by the lamp

*

L'espérance et la nue
Ombrelle sur l'oiseau c'est l'idée
Inespérée visage allégé beau théâtre

Ombrelle un peu d'un oui sur ce visage
Aimé parfois par son épaule c'est théâtre
De terre disant l'amour si je dis

Le mot confié, la ligne du sein cru
Formé des liens de tout cela contenu
Dans une idée :   ô théâtre ô nuageuse

*

Je dis l'esprit de neige avant mourir
De neige étant les formes dans l'esprit
La forme ayant désavoué la neige

Le vide étant l'arbitre en la douleur
De la saisie d'ici par figure
Avant l'avoir d'aucune forme prise

Sinon les yeux de désaveu
De celui qu'une fatigue a fait de neige
Et que recueille avant mourir une pure

*

Soufflant sur l'arbre emmuré dans le souffle
Lune Casquée Chef-d'œuvre ô Gorgerin

L'éclair de chevaucher dans l'œil
: Arquée par le chant excessif

– Tombe une lampe en feu
Dans le jardin d'une eau de ténèbre
Par le froid consentie

*

Hope and high cloud
A parasol over the bird is the unhoped-for
Idea a face lightened fine theatre

A parasol something of a yes upon this face
Loved at times by her shoulder it is earthly
Theatre speaking love if I speak

The entrusted word, the line of her raw bosom
Formed from the bonds of everything contained
In an idea: of theatre oh she of cloud

*

I speak the spirit of snow before dying
Of snow being the shapes in the mind
Form having disavowed snow

The void being judge in the pain
Of the seizure of here through figure
Before the having of no seized form

Except for the eyes of disavowal
Of him whom fatigue has turned to snow
And who is gathered up before dying by a woman pure

*

Blowing upon the tree walled up in breath
Helmeted Moon Masterpiece oh Throat-piece

The lightning flash of riding in the eye
: She arched over by excessive song

– There falls a fiery lamp
In the garden of some darkened water
Consented to by the cold

*

Oiseaux recueillis d'une neige
Entourés d'une lampe
Et disparus

dans l'interstice entre le souffle et le

*

Sans arc, guerrier du souffle
Contre – parmi – le souffle. Arc
    , du souffle

En souvenir de l'herbe, à cause
De cela par quoi l'herbe, à cause
Du nom de cela : l'herbe –

ô arc. ô
Armée   Oh
– Cela cela pourtant :
Le chien d'interruption à minuit

*

Accrue dans le feu l'herbe
A dénaturé l'origine et cuit le pain
– Profonde entre les cils

Œil enseigné de cils
Ou blé où se désigne
Le blé des larmes

Feu est raison   l'herbe
N'est pas le feu mais le déni de l'herbe
À la fin déracinée par oubli

*

Gathered birds of a snowing
Surrounded by a lamp
And disappeared

into the gap between breath and

*

Bowless, warrior of breath
Against – amidst – breath. Bow
        , of breath

In memory of the grass, because
Of that via which grass, because
Of the name of that : grass –

oh bow. oh
Army   Ah
– That that nevertheless :
The change of watch dog at midnight

*

Increased in fire the grass
Has denatured origin and baked bread
– Deep between the eyelashes

Eye taught by eyelashes
Or wheat where is designated
The wheat of tears

Fire is reason   grass
Is not fire but the denial of grass
Finally uprooted through forgetfulness

*

Obscure lampe enserrée de fourmis
Pour l'épousée des ronces
En serpentine terre ayant talon

Puis vive lampe inexpliquée des ronces
Tenace au lit des ronces
Avivées par l'approche obscure de l'amant

Instrumentistes purs
Sont les amants, donnant
Leur bien (un scarabée) au crépuscule

*

Et l'épervier
Est arraché au sens
: Du bec et de la serre

Ceci dans l'arbre : une
Fiévreuse de substance
Au pied de l'arbre, (…)

Ou précision de l'arbre :
        Contour.
Plaisir plaisir de l'épervier dans le sens !

*

Par l'herbe, par le vœu de l'herbe l'herbe
A dénoué les nœuds

Je, dérivé du sens
Outil d'une lumière
Servante sous les mouches

Ô lampe éteinte – amour,
Et comme amour avivé près du sein
Qui sait le sens (…) et prie.

*

Obscure lamp encompassed by ants
For the wedded woman of brambles
Having heel within the serpentine earth

Then unexplained live lamp of brambles
Clinging to the bed of brambles
Quickened by the lover's obscure approach

Pure instrumentalists
Lovers are, giving
Their wealth (a beetle) to dusk

*

And the sparrow-hawk
Is torn away from meaning
: By beak and talon.

This in the tree : a woman
Fevered with substance
At the foot of the tree, (...)

Or the tree's preciseness :
        Circumference.
Pleasure pleasure of the sparrow-hawk in meaning!

*

Through grass, through the vow of grass grass
Has undone the knots

I, off-shoot of meaning
Implement of a light
Servant-woman beneath the flies

oh lamp extinguished – love
And like love quickened near the bosom
That knows meaning (...) and prays.

*

Herbe d'herbe   visage
Annexé à la rosée d'herbe
Puis la rosée retirée, et le visage.

Au sol arraché, ange-dire
        : visage obscurci d'herbe
Aigle friable et grand d'une herbe sur

Ce qui fut et ce qui sera, rocheuse roche
Ou robe ôtée de femme à plis jolis avec
Au joint des jambes, sang (…) et la rosée

*

Comme arc – puis comme arc.
Arc immobile
: éclat.

Éclat, ortie du cri
Dans une brume de brume, dont le froid
Se forme en arbre et fait le fruit

L'arc et le cri de l'arc
Entre ceci et cela : l'eau de l'arbre
Est façonnée dans l'amour la funèbre

*

Grass of grass   face
Appended to the grassy dew
Then dew withdrawn, and the face

From the earth torn, angel-speech
    : face darkened by grass
Great brittle eagle of a grass above

What was and what will be, rocky rock
Or woman's dress removed with its pretty pleats with
In the crease of legs, blood (...) and dew

*

Like a bow – then like a bow.
Motionless bow
: splinter of light.

Splendour, the scream's nettle
In a mist of mist, whose cold
Shapes itself into a tree and makes fruit

The bow and the scream of the bow
Between this and that : the water of the tree
Is fashioned in love funereal water

*

Arbres de ma lignée   ô patience
Comme herbe et bœufs de terre
Serrant le bleu d'éternité archange
– Et quel archange, bœufs, cornes pures,
Arbres da ma lignée ?

Amants
Jeûnant par faim – de lin et d'herbe !
: Labour touchant beauté de lit. Mort :
Enfance déjouant les nids

Arbres de ma lignée avant le sens,
Les bœufs ayant paru et disparu
Sous l'été vert et gagné leur empire
Par les mouches formées   Arbres dits
Et devenus arbres devant le sens

*

Trees of my lineage   oh patience
Like grass and earth oxen
Holding tight the blue of archangel eternity
– And what archangel, oxen, pure horns,
Trees of my lineage?

Lovers
Fasting out of hunger – upon flax and grass!
: Tilling touching bedded beauty. Death :
Childhood outwitting nests

Trees of my lineage before meaning,
The oxen having appeared and disappeared
Beneath the green summer and reached their empire
Through created flies   Trees spoken
And become trees in the face of meaning

*

de Inversion de l'arbre et du silence (1980)

: de ceci, lampe nouée amoureusement
L'huile d'une parole proférée
La nuit tombée sur une lampe, la
Langue en cette lampe a racine

Le froid muettement
D'avant (après) le nœud des lampes, flamme
En cette lampe par ces nœuds déliée

Et qui parlera, lampe, mal-
Gré le souffle qui sur   elle   soufflera
Langue parlant de lampe
La femme assise à l'écouter obscure
Tenant sur ses genoux genoux ses mains obscures

*

Lampe la joue dévorée par les arbres
En ce jardin de terre, celui-là
Consolidant le feu

Non-feu se repliant dans une lampe
Dite et redite, soudain proférée
Et posée là sur la table du jour

Attendant, table, le bois et les liaisons
De l'être à demi fidèle à l'arbre
Au feu à demi, par la lampe endeuillé

*

from Inversion of Tree and Silence (1980)

: of this, lamp knotted lovingly
The oil of speech uttered
Night fallen upon a lamp,
Language within this lamp finds root

The cold wordlessly
From before (after) the knot of lamps, flame
Within this lamp through these knots unbound

And lamp poised to speak, des-
Pite the breath that upon   it   will blow
Language speaking of lamp
The woman sitting listening to it in darkness
Holding on her knees knees her darkened hands

*

Lamp the cheek devoured by the trees
Within this garden of earth, its other
Strengthening the fire

No-fire folding back upon a lamp
Spoken over and over, suddenly uttered
And placed there upon the table of day

Table, waiting, for the wood and the linkages
Of being, half-faithful to the tree
Half to the fire, cast into mourning by the lamp

*

Je dis l'esprit de neige avant mourir
De neige étant les formes dans l'esprit
La forme ayant désavoué la neige

Le vide étant l'arbitre en la douleur
De la saisie d'ici par figure
Avant l'avoir d'aucune forme prise

Sinon les yeux de désaveu
De celui qu'une fatigue a fait de neige
Et que recueille avant mourir une pure

*

Orage du silence
Éclairant en tours et détours le nuage

Oliveraie !

Par l'herbe :

: La lampe de l'unicité de l'herbe

Voilà
        sous la saisie
L'impur et le voilé

*

I speak the spirit of snow before death
Of snow being all forms in spirit
Form having disavowed snow

The void being judge in the pain
Of seizure here through figuration
Before the having of no assumed form

But for the eyes of disavowal
Of him that tiredness has made snow-like
And that before death she who is pure gathers up

*

Storm of silence
Lighting up in twists and turns the cloud

Olive grove!

Through the grass :

: The lamp of the uniqueness of grass

There
        beneath their seizure
Lie the impure and the veiled

*

Herbe d'herbe   visage
Annexé à la rosée d'herbe
Puis la rosée retirée, et le visage

Au sol arraché, ange-dire
     : visage obscurci d'herbe
Aigle friable et grand d'une herbe sur

Ce qui fut et ce qui sera, rocheuse roche
Ou robe ôtée de femme à plis jolis avec
Au joint des jambes, sang (...) et la rosée

*

Lampe éveillée dans l'herbe
Selon l'espoir du sens
Et recueillie dans la lumière double

Ô épervier irradiant le dieu du sens
(Les serres serrant le sens)
– Le trèfle des prairies fixant l'envers du sens

D'aucun sens est le sens – dit le sens
Allumé en foyer d'oubli ce peu d'herbe
Par mouvement de prairies dans la mort

*

108

Grass of grass   face
Attached to grassy dew
Then the dew withdrawn, and the face

From the ground snatched, angel-saying
        : face darkened with grass
Great and brittle eagle of grass above

What was and what will be, rocky rock
Or woman's robe removed with lovely folds with
At the joining of legs, blood (...) and moist dew

*

Lamp awakened in the grass
According to the hope for meaning
And gathered up in the twin light

Oh sparrow-hawk irradiating the god of meaning
(The talons grasping meaning tight)
– The clover of meadows staring at the other side of meaning

Of no meaning is meaning – called meaning
Lit up like a hotbed of oblivion this grassy minimum
Via movement of meadows in death

*

Poupée de la douleur de la substance
Dans la douleur et tout le blé
– Ô recueillie dans le songe du blé

Sombre lampe d'été serrant le blé
Contre son corps de pauvre : tous les cils
Du blé pour un œil d'oiseau sur le blé

Or la lampe a rompu la mesure du blé
Et tout le blé enfin est nul, toute substance
Brûle une idée de main dans le blé

*

Puis le buste est remis à la pauvreté d'herbe
Par les anges de la dérision du nom
En attente du nom orné, avant l'herbe

Ô main ô dessaisie
Formant   saisie   la lampe des bleuets
Renversée dans l'antiquité de l'herbe

Fin commune : écriture
Illisible, lisible au lecteur d'arbres
…Ô lampe des bleuets dans ce théâtre !

*

Doll of the pain of substance
In pain itself and all that is wheat
– Oh gathered up in the daydream of wheat

Dark summer lamp grasping tight the wheat
Against its poor man's body : all the eyelashes
Of wheat for a bird's gaze across the wheat

Now the lamp has broken open the measure of wheat
And all wheat is finally null, all substance
Burns a notion of hand in wheat

*

Then the arms and breast are returned to grassy poverty
By the angels of derision of name
In waiting for a name adorned, before grass

Oh hand oh dispossessed
Forming   by possession   the lamp of blueberries
Cast down in the ancientness of grass

Common end : writing
Illegible, legible to the reader of trees
…Oh lamp of blueberries in this theatre !

*

La stratégie : cela contre le chant
Par discipline et par amour de l'herbe
Brume de terre : cela, sauvant l'herbe
En sa nature d'herbe ; arc est le chant

Et comme espace avec les arcs l'ange
Formant autour de soi brume de terre
Et tenant l'arc au point formé de terre
D'où lèvera, arbre et herbe, cela :

Enfant dormeur puis endormi dans l'herbe
Sous l'arc et sous la flèche, gain de terre
Pour l'ange, ô déshabillé d'une substance
D'aucune terre. Stratégie : herbe des arcs.

*

À la bifurcation du corps et de l'esprit
Est ce peu d'herbe herbeuse : étonnée
Par l'ange obscur de terre

Or qui par l'ange énoncera le vœu
De l'herbe inhabitée comme maison
Impure, l'épée de nature en elle ?

Unique impur oiseau sur le visible
Distribué en pauvres fruits. L'épée
A désuni l'herbe et l'herbe – forçant le vœu

*

The strategy : that which is against the song
Out of discipline and out of love of grass
Earth mist : that which is, saving grass
Within its grassy nature ; the song is bow

And by way of space with the bows the angel
Forming about itself earth mist
And grasping the bow at the point created from earth
From which will rise, tree and grass, that which is :

Child sleeper then asleep in the grass
Beneath the bow and beneath the arrow, the earth won over
By the angel, oh undressed in a substance
Of no earth. Strategy : grass of bows.

*

At the forking of body and spirit
Is this minimum of grassy grass : amazed
By the dark earth angel

Now who by the angel will state the desire
Of grass uninhabited like a house
Impure, the sword of nature within it ?

Unique pure bird above the visible
Shared out like humble fruits. The sword
Has riven grass and grass – forcing desire

*

...Puis la fulguration. La joliesse
Retenue en perfection du sens
Qui fait l'oiseau fulgurant dans la beauté

Brûlantes serres, fulguration de l'oiseau
Détruit par excès de sens, avivé
Par le sens – au durcissement du sens

Sens est l'oiseau, serres non dessaisies
D'une joliesse accrue dans la beauté
Accrue : dominant les géraniums

*

Joliesse en palpitation de cendre
Autour de l'extrême lampe enracinée
Dans l'évidence de racines, lampe
Extrême à peine – feuilles devenues noires

Retenant, pur cela, l'idée
De la lumière à cela attachée
Qui s'ouvre lampe, lumière œuvrée de mort
Établie, outil ou épée, près des racines

Impur cela, racine enracinée
Dans l'ambiguë terre, lampe de terre
Jolie de jolie beauté, outil
Enterré et lumière emmurée dans

*

… Then fulguration. Prettiness
Retained as perfection of meaning
That gives fulguration to bird in beauty

Burning talons, fulgurating bird
Destroyed by excess of meaning, quickened
Through meaning – to the hardening of meaning

Meaning is bird, talons not dispossessed
Of an increased prettiness in beauty
Increased : dominating geraniums

*

Prettiness like quivering of ash
About the extreme lamp rooted
In the blatancy of roots, lamp
Barely extreme – leaves become black

Retaining, pure thatness, the idea
Of light bound to that
Which opens like a lamp, worked light of death
Established, tool or sword, by the roots

Impure thatness, root rooted
In ambiguous earth, lamp of earth
Pretty with pretty beauty, tool
Buried and light walled up in

*

Loques de force dans l'esprit, ongles
Brillant de l'éclat de rien, brillant
D'une intuition comme rose d'arçons

En espérance d'une guerre – oh! criant
Sa forte soie aux ombres de l'esprit
Multipliant l'amour et les armées

Ô défendue par espoir d'espérance
Brillant de rien, armes tombées
Quand vient la nuit, et le blé, lampe sobre

*

Le blé du blé est le blé des amants
Cousins du blé, herbe d'approche
– Nouée.

Lampe nouée, lampe du blé, aux marges de
Ce champ mental, lié au blé
Liée lampe liée à l'approche

Amants, le blé les sauve
À cause de la pauvreté de cela
Qui les approche et qui défait leur lampe

*

Rags of strength in the mind, fingernails
Shining with the splendour of nothingness, shining
With an intuition like a saddle-bow rose

Hoping for war – oh! shouting out
Its strong silkiness to the shadows of the mind
Proliferating love and armies

Oh she forbidden out of hope for hope
Shining with nothingness, weapons fallen limp
When night comes, and wheat, sober lamp

*

Wheat of wheat is the wheat of lovers
Cousins to wheat, grass for a drawing near
– Knotted.

Knotted lamp, lamp of wheat, in the margins of
This mental field, bound to wheat
Bound lamp bound to a drawing near

Lovers, saved by wheat
Because of the poverty of that
Which draws them close and undoes their lamp

*

Destruction de la poupée Destruction de l'ange Des-
Truction de leur maison, de leur chambre
Afin de sauver l'eau dans la maison

Pour le salut immatériel de l'âme
Ajoutée à la nudité, pur dehors
Enraciné dans la rupture et dans la feinte

Afin de sauver l'eau portée. Afin
: Que la maison soit dure. Afin
: Que l'arbre vert soit l'arbitre de la mort

*

Œillet pâle en limpidité de l'être
Hôte d'une grâce infinie
Autour – saisissement – du pur cela

Comme plus pur : accompli. Pure
Réserve
Affleurant comme l'eau à l'eau de l'œil

Œillet impur des cils ! Désir
Désirant par désir
Qui fait briller l'œil le plus proche

*

Destruction of the doll Destruction of the angel De-
Struction of their house, of their room
So as to save the water of the house

For the immaterial saving of the soul
Added to nakedness, pure externalness
Rooted in breakage and in feint

So as to save the water borne up. So
: That the house may be tough. So
: That the green tree may be the arbiter of death

*

Pale carnation like being's limpidness
Host of some infinite grace
About – seizure – pure thatness

As purer : achieved. Pure
Reserve
Surfacing like water in the watering of eyes

Impure carnation of eyelashes ! Desire
Desiring out of desire
That brings brilliance to the nearest eye

*

Fruits surgis d'écriture
Éternellement / fruits
Endormis dans le sein de Hölderlin

Non cueillis non respirés
Plus profonds autour de leur nom : puisant
Dans la nuit de leur nom leur pauvre nom

Fruits, ils furent. Nommés : ils furent –
: Une fois. Une fois
Respirés respirés par l'ange de leur Nom

*

Destruction du nom et de l'image
Face au fini visage
Ô veuve ornée devenue forme d'arbre

: Ornée du fer des ombres
Toute patrie fermée de tous ses arbres
Et son désert, menaçantes étoiles

Destruction des ornements par les veuves
Restituant le nu jardin, leur corps
Étant étroit

*

Fruits of writing surging forth
Eternally / fruits
Fallen asleep in the bosom of Hölderlin

Not picked not breathed
Deeper about their names : drawing
From the night of their names their poor names

Fruits, they were. Named : they were –
: Once. Once
Breathed breathed by the angel of their Names

*

Destruction of name and image
Before the finite face
Oh adorned widow become treed form

: Adorned with the iron of shadows
Every homeland shut off by all its trees
And its desert, stars threatening

Destruction of embellishments by widows
Restoring the naked garden, their bodies
Close and cramped

*

Tumultueuse lampe
En la beauté de neige et de parole
Effrayée : mots de neige

Neige, et le liseron : ambiguë
Bouche
– Ongles, absolus par la mort

Parole étroite ou sourde
La femme au sein vivant qui se referme
Face éblouie de larmes

*

Aveuglées par la joue du froid
Douces larmes
De ce visage entre les cils

Approches
: Noire terre
Aux fins de restitution écrite

Aux arbres! À la brume,
À l'herbe, à tous exercices formant fruit,
Aux eaux de lampe vive,

Larmes (vos joues) poupées pulvérisées

*

Lamp of tumult
Within the beauty of snow and speech
In frightened awe : words of snow

Snow, and the convolvulus : ambiguous
Mouth
– Fingernails, absolute through death

Cramped or dull speech
Woman of living bosom closing upon itself
Face dazzled with tears

*

Blinded by the cheek of coldness
Sweet tears
Of this face between eyelashes

Approaches
: Black earth
Seeking written restitution

To trees ! To mist,
To grass, to all exercises forming fruit,
To the live lamp waters,

Tears (your cheeks) dolls ground to powder

*

Lampe fraîche à feuillage
Accru, enterrant – brûlure – toute lampe
Dans la beauté de terre

Amoureuse approchée
Appauvrie lampe fraîche
Auprès du corps réel

Inscrite à des extrémités d'écriture
En espérance accrue du corps réel
Dans un jardin de terre

*

Et la douleur de l'esprit jusqu'à l'arbre
À travers la totalité des nœuds
Et les nœuds des nuages
Les nœuds de la substance jusqu'à l'herbe
À travers les difficultés de l'herbe

Lampe
Lampe brillante
Brillante – et solide
Porteuse de maturité dans les fruits
Comme le lait dans le sein pur, le déchirant

Et les nœuds des nuages
À travers la totalité des nœuds
Jusqu'au nœud de la lampe très obscure
Établie dans le lieu du lieu – sous l'herbe
, L'habitée. L'arbre a bleui dans la poussière bleue.

*

Cool lamp with its foliage
Enhanced, burying – burning – every lamp
In the earthen beauty

Loving impoverished
Cool lamp drawn close
By the real body

Inscribed lamp at writing's extremities
In enhanced hope of the real body
In a garden of earth

*

And the mind's pain to the very tree
Through the full sum of knots
And the knottings of clouds
The knots of substance to the very grass
Through the difficulties of grass

Lamp
Shining lamp
Shining – and firm
Bearing matureness in fruits
Like milk in the pure breast, tearing it open

And the knottings of clouds
Through the full sum of knots
To the very knot of the most dark lamp
Established in the place of place – beneath the grass
, In-dwelled. The tree has turned blue in the blue dust.

*

L'infiguré, le maître de la lampe
En ardente maison
Comme douleur incréée de colombe

Qu'il soit le fils des formes
Dans la maison-maison rendue limpide
Par la brûlure allégée du jasmin

Ô maître de la lampe
: Médiation d'une colombe incendiée
Au ciel innommé des figures

*

L'infiguré, le fils de la figure
Comme femme aux maïs
En qui l'infiguré prend figure

Obscurcie de nuages
Qu'elle dorme, oh qu'elle dorme !
Approchée par des larmes

À cause d'une absence de mourir
Est l'idée de l'oiseau
Plus pure que les effets de l'arc

*

The unfigured, the master of the lamp
Within burning house
Like uncreated pain of dove

May he be the son of forms
In the house-house rendered limpid
By the lightened burning of jasmine

Oh master of the lamp
: Mediation of a dove afire
In the unnamed sky of figures

*

The unfigured, the son of figuration
Like a woman with maize
Within whom the unfigured takes shape

Obscured by clouds
Let her sleep, oh let her sleep!
Drawn close through tears

Because of an absence of dying
Is the idea of the bird
Purer than the effects of the bow

*

Orphelin est prénom du merle, dit le merle

Très noir d'avoir dicté
Le non-blé bleuâtre du blé, ce théâtre
D'un peu de matin faible

Non-blé du blé
Et chant d'aveugle neige
Errant aux rives comédiennes

*

Cela fut dit : nulle œuvre de l'été
Ne sera blé consolé de parole
À cause du retrait de la parole

Ce peu de fruit aux arbres
Est l'arc, est le fruit de la parole
Maison de tombe, jarre

Cela fut dit : par excès de saison
Sera le fruit du fruit, presque nommé
Par référence pierreuse aux bleuets

*

Orphan is the blackbird's first name, says the blackbird

Most black from dictating
The bluish no-wheat of wheat, the theatre
Of some faint morning minimum

No-wheat of wheat
And song of blind snow
Wandering along the theatrical riverbanks

*

That was said : no summer's work
Will be solaced wheat of speech
Because of the withdrawal of speech

This minimum of fruit on the trees
Is the bow, is the fruit of speech
Tomb-dwelling, great urn

That was said : out of seasonal excess
Will be the fruit of fruit, almost named
Through stony reference to blueberries

*

Le livre, le rompu, l'indécidé
En absolu théâtre
Et la poupée de son cri s'est éloignée

Voilée de vin, voilée de pauvre blé
Aux fins du pain inexpliqué, aux fins
, Livre enterré, du blé qui sera blé

Livre enterré dans la terre du livre
Comme poupée séparée de son cri
À l'aube, au tranchant vieilli des charrues

*

Et les amants de l'arc
Ont tué la poupée au cri de l'origine
Et touché au sensible sens la fillette

La sourde à la parole
Épousée par le blé de la parole
Ayant mûri par vœu dans l'amour

À ce blé les amants
Ont touché, à ce blé
La paume de leur main a disparu

*

The book, broken, indeterminate
Like absolute theatre
And the doll has left its cry behind

Veiled with wine, veiled with humble wheat
In the service of unexplained bread, in the service
, Buried book, of wheat that will be wheat

Book buried in the earth of the book
Like a doll separated from its cry
At dawn, upon the aged blade of ploughs

*

And the lovers of the bow
Have killed the doll and its primordial cry
And touched in her sensitive meaning the young girl

She who is deaf to speech
Wedded to the wheat of speech
Having ripened through desire in love

This wheat lovers
Have touched, this wheat
The palms of their hands have disappeared

*

Entre monde et le monde
Avec plante, en animal de beauté
Broutant, sein de l'esprit, le très pur

Le nu. Le désassemblé. L'à peine
Approché. Le
Venteux. Le nul.

Plus loin sont fruits

Cernant la faim

*

Between world and the world
With plant, like an animal of beauty
Grazing, bosom of the mind, upon the most pure

The naked. The disassembled. The barely
Approached. The
Windswept. The null.

Further yet are fruits

Hemming in hunger

*

de Colombe Aquiline (1983)

Armes de terre et les dahlias de larmes
Dans l'incendie brûlant l'épée des cils
Limpide aussi par larmes

À cause, cils, de la domination
Des larmes sur l'esprit de femme rouge
En orpheline terre

Ô pluie parfaite entre nymphe et racine
Le corps de femme assemblant guerre
Ses bras debout et ses amants dormant

*

Dahlia de l'air seul
Brûlant contre la nuit des murs
Dans l'air à fin immense

Le rien, ses jardinets,
Où des papillons brillent
Amoureusement – brillent

Comme lampe rompue
Épouse en sa robe ôtée essentielle
Substance fille, et ses éclairements

*

from Eagle Dove (1983)

Weapons of earth and the dahlias of tears
In the searing inferno the sword of eyelashes
Limpid too through tears

Because, lashes, of the dominance
Of tears over red woman's spirit
Within orphaned earth

Oh perfect rain between nymph and root
Woman's body gathering war
Her arms held high and her lovers sleeping

*

Dahlia of air alone
Burning against the night of walls
In the immense-purposed air

The nothingness, its little gardens,
Where butterflies shine bright
With love – shine bright

Like a broken lamp
Bride in her dress removed essential
Girlish substance, and its illuminations

*

Lumière illuminée par lumière
Ses os parfois visibles
Par dispersion du corps soyeux dans l'herbe

Tremblant dans l'eau de ce qu'il est rompant ses robes
Sur l'autre corps au pied de sang
Et toute fourche en lui illuminée

Brillant triangle dans l'esprit
Herbe enflammée
Par sacre de l'esprit dans ce massacre

*

Nuage – et les ornements des nuages
Lampe de l'être ô effrayée
Native et pulvérisée et froide

À cause de l'immensité du verdoiement
Autour de l'arbre d'une neige
Toute brûlure en lui formant fruit

Ombre de femme en sa nudité venteuse
Son enfance aux aguets
Fille d'amour promise aux tables vives

*

Light lit up by light
Her bones at times visible
Through dispersal of the silken body in the grass

Trembling in the water of what it is breaking apart her robes
Upon the other bloody-footed body
And every pitchfork in it illuminated

Shining triangle in the mind
Grass put to flames
By consecration of spirit in this slaughter

*

Cloud – and the adornments of clouds
Lamp of being oh how awed in fright
Inborn and ground to powder and cold

By the vastness of greening
Around the tree of a snowing
All burning within forming fruit

Shadow of woman in her windswept nakedness
Her childhood on the watch
Daughter of love promised to the living tables

*

L'absolue robe, la brûlante, l'agnelle
Et son enfance rouge
Et son corps éclaté de femme – rouge

En mélange avec le raisin, le dormant vin
De sa nature indésirée ou désirante
Et désirée d'esprit par colombe

En mélange avec le raisin elle chante,
Ses entrailles brûlant au crépuscule
Parce qu'elles vivent, ses longs yeux devenus fous

*

Ses yeux devenus fous
Un soir de feux et d'herbe
Elle va, son visage

Avec le liséré des larmes et les cils
Donnés à l'ange de tout froid
– Sa plume, flamme ouverte

Elle va, son visage
À l'arrivée au port qui brûle
Se défait en immense cendre

*

The absolute robe, she that burns, the ewe-lamb
And her red childhood
And her bright-shattered woman's body – red

Mixed with the grape, the sleeping wine
Of her nature undesired or desiring
And desired of spirit by dove

Mixed with the grape she sings,
Her bowels burning in the dusk
Because they live on, her long eyes turned to madness

*

Her eyes turned to madness
On an evening of fires and grass
She goes forth, her face.

With the edging of tears and her eyelashes
Given to the angel of all cold
– Its feathering an open flame

She goes forth, her face
As she reaches the burning harbour
Is undone in immense ash

*

de **Nuage avec des voix** (1984)

Près des fourmis de ces montagnes
Sous la beauté de l'esprit sous le malheur
De l'esprit et sous l'arbre

Établi dans la viduité du vide
: Plus silencieux que silence le corbeau
N'a plus de nom dans la nullité
Nulle

Dieu des fourmis dans la rougeur
D'une contrée   Dieu d'agneau beau
Aux portes éclatées

*

L'esprit –   de terre
Brûle :
Yeux de larmes

        Aurore,
Enseigne ce peu d'eau

            *

Et quel esprit
Au tranchant des violettes ?

Précise, respirante

Ô pluie…
À vérifier le loup !

            *

Tranchant de l'œil

        : verdoiement du souffle

        , et nœuds d'herbe

*

from Cloud with Voices (1984)

Close by the ants of these mountains
Beneath the mind's beauty beneath the unhappiness
Of mind and beneath the tree

Established in the viduity of the void
: More silent than silence the raven
Is no longer in the null
Nullness

God of ants in the redness
Of a land   God of lamb lovely
At the gates burst asunder

*

The spirit –   of earth
Is burning :
Eyes of tears

      Dawn,
Teach this bit of water

     *

And what spirit
At the cutting edge of violets ?

Exact, breathing

Oh rain…
Verifying the wolf !

    *

Cutting edge of the eye

     : greening of breath

     , and knots of grass

*

La robe de prière
Épouse au brûlant corps
Espérant le tranchant

Toute beauté
Costumée dans l'esprit
Par l'insecte des larmes

Comme une lampe incréée presque nocturne
Pour l'épousée de terre

*

Le lion de Son visage
Dans la brûlure imbrûlée du vent

Et la lumière n'est personne

*

Et je te dis l'enfant de la nuée
Par la douleur de l'arbre de substance
Et son ruisseau d'aveugle

Par la fourmi par des montagnes par le songe
Par l'ange et le tourbillon des forces
Costumant Dieu de grandes fleurs nulles

Ô cœur d'étroite épingle
Avec l'oiseau de plumes
Au ciel soudain paré de parures

*

The robe of prayer
Spouse of burning body
In hope of the cutting edge

Every beauty
Clothed in the mind
By the insect of tears

Like an uncreated near-nocturnal lamp
For the wedded woman of earth

*

The lion of His face
In the unburned burning of the wind

And the light is not anyone

*

And I say to you the child of the clouds
By the pain of the tree of substance
And its blind man's stream

By the ant by mountains by dream
By the angel and the whirlwind of forces
Clothing God in great flowers of nullness

Oh tight-pinned heart
With the bird of feathers
In the sky decked sudden with ornament

*

Atrocité des fleurs d'ici
Par tout ce rouge et l'assemblée des insectes
Tous les violons devenus cendre
Aveugle et sourd leur délice
Sur les chemins sinueux du Très Limpide
Une montagne
Allant s'éteindre avec ses libellules

*

Fiancée des libellules
Lumière en gestation métaphysique
Par un jour d'apparences
Le vent propice a dégagé des larmes
Les voici accusées
À cause de l'esprit en qui elles vont
Errer sur l'absolu des structures
Pour notre amour ô barque ô allégée

*

Et le feu a brûlé dans la substance
Comme cri aux terrasses
Ô draperie, d'un cri, se défaisant
Déchirée dans la blancheur des terrasses

Et la barque a brûlé dans la substance
Sous une pierre voûtée immatérielle
Enfants parfois dormeurs
Leur visage alourdi dans la flambée

Et le feu a brûlé dans la substance
Ciels asséchés allant au réel
À la fin restituant une larme
Larme larme
Disparue recomposée disparue
Pour l'égarement des libellules

*

Atrocity of the flowers amongst us
Through the redness everywhere and the assembly of insects
All violins become ash
Blind and deaf their delight
Upon the sinuous paths of the Most Limpid
A mountain
Falling to extinction with its dragonflies

*

Fiancée of dragonflies
Light in metaphysical gestation
Upon a day of appearances
The favourable wind has loosened tears
Here they are, heightened
By the spirit within which they seek
To wander over the absoluteness of structures
For our love, oh ship oh lightened one

*

And the fire has burned in the substance
Like a crying out upon the terraces
Oh drapings, with a cry, unclothed
Torn apart in the whiteness of terraces

And the ship has burned in the substance
Beneath an unsubstantial vault of stone
Children sometimes sleepyheads
Their faces weighed down in the blaze

And the fire has burned in the substance
Parched skies drifting to reality
Finally restoring a tear
Tear tear
Gone recombined gone
For the bewilderment of dragonflies

*

Enfants dans la brûlure
Fils d'enracinement par sommeil
La brume a décousu l'orage
Par médiation de la complexité céleste
À cause d'une tuerie

                              Antique
Est la vapeur céleste : irraisonnée,
Habillée d'herbe, et d'herbe; habillée
D'insectes dans le devenir de l'insecte

Flamme étalée dans l'herbe
Et découverte ou définie par la brume
Complice d'arbre et de raison
Avant la tuerie éblouie
Avivée par la singerie du fleuve

*

Merle ébloui par le buisson
Enterré dans la flamme
Lampe d'air obsédée
À cause d'une tuerie limpide

: Entre deux pas elle tremble

Flamme éloignée des mouches
Sous le verre inaltéré du soupçon

... Sont-ils vapeur diurne
Compliquée de pavots ?

... Et leur barque de terre enfin rompue
Et leur enfance ?

*

Children in the burning
Threads of rooting via sleep
The mist has unsewn the storm
By mediation of celestial complexity
On account of some slaughter

Ancient
Is the celestial haze : unreasoned,
Dressed in grass, and grass; dressed
With insects in the becoming of the insect

Flame displayed in the grass
And uncovered or defined by the mist
Abettor of tree and of reason
Before the dazzled slaughter
Quickened by the river's aping

*

Blackbird dazzled by the bush
Buried in the flame
Lamp of air obsessed
On account of a limpid slaughtering

: Between two strides it flickers

Distanced flame of flies
Under the unaltered glass of suspicion

… Are they diurnal haze
Complicated by poppies ?

… And their ship of earth finally broken
And their childhood ?

*

Le blé de seigneurie
Par immanence et par idéation
Selon le fruit de l'interrogation du sable
Est préservé de tous bourdonnements
Et l'on salue la perfectibilité des astres
L'un d'eux, très sinueux !
Dans l'air brillant éclairé de pavots
Au seuil de la beauté des morts

                             Le blé !

Seigneur de l'Est et de l'Ouest
Aux établissements. Brille
Sa lampe ici adressée aux bleuâtres
Libres lumières errantes des pavots...

Plus forts pavots
Au seuil de l'origine
Que terre et lampe et nocturne beauté
De celles qui sont
Assises
Sans respirer

*

Ô mon amour le dernier mot « s'éteindre »
Est dans la rue en flamboiement de flamme
L'amour l'accueille et l'aime :
Il est le pigeon de son cœur

Lampe lampe de brise
Dans les pleurs par-delà le froid,
Maison vide éclairée
Du pauvre amour aux méandres du fleuve

Par les brûlures de la rue l'enfant
Portant ses mains de brise
Donne aux manies du feu un visage
Et brille aussi au confluent du froid

*

148

The wheat of seigneury
By immanence and by ideation
According to the fruit of the querying of sand
Is preserved from all buzzings
And we greet the perfectibility of stars
One amongst them, most sinuous !
In the brilliant air lit with poppies
At the threshold of the beauty of the dead.

Wheat !

Lord of the East and the West
In the settlements. Shining here
Is its lamp upon the blue-tinted
Free-wandering lights of poppies...

Poppies stronger
At the threshold of origin
Than earth and lamp and nocturnal beauty
Of women who are
Sitting
Breathless

*

Oh my love the final word 'extinction'
Is upon the streets in blazing of flame
Love gives it welcome and love :
It is the pigeon of its heart

Lamp lamp of breeze
In the tears beyond the cold,
Empty house lighted
By poor love in the river's meanderings

Through the streets' burnings the child
Bearing its hands of breeze
Gives face to the manias of fire
And shines too at the confluence of the cold

*

de **Lecture d'une femme** (1987)

Ce pays détruit – ces toits noirs... La mer en face : éclatante. Un ange blessé traverse tout cela et sa poudre malheureuse, et, dans la poussière, il traîne invisiblement son aile démantelée. L'ange serait-il là pour camoufler d'un peu de panache métaphysique la déraison inexplicable des choses, leur dislocation ? Et les hommes, que des forces agitent et qui croient que ces forces, c'est en eux qu'elles prennent naissance et qu'ainsi ils les gouvernent – pantins fougueusement portés sous les lustres d'un théâtre et qu'ensorcèlent ces feux d'un instant – les voici déjà repris par le mouvement renversé et les voici, désarmés, prestige éteint, qui font place à la neuve foule et à ses nouveaux dieux allant au néant. Ainsi vont les forces. Seuls d'aveugles aveugles croient aux théories, aux théorèmes, à ce puissant cheval de bronze qu'enfourchent, sur les places publiques, les conquérants de bronze. Le monde n'est que fragilités et que délicatesses, et la nature aussi dans ses raffinements le moins visiblement naturés, et l'homme aussi avec son ordinaire, et sa femme. Tout cela qui n'est pas de bronze, mais de joli bonheur en arc-en-ciel, est soumis au règne des forces, j'entends, peut-être, à celui des fous du Roi. Et si lui-même, le Roi, s'il était fou ? Ainsi allait ma rêverie, sur ce pays de mort qui fut le mien. Et que j'aimais. Ce pays où vint souffrir la planète entière, par compassion. Car, moi le mort, dès que je quitte du regard Héléna qui se sait et ne se sait pas observée, je prends dans mon œil absolu l'entière planète et je la sais, moi à qui la science enfin est venue, faible, et vivante, et capable de transparence.

Cela, que j'énonce ainsi, est mystérieux, je le vois bien, et, peut-être, par la suite, me sera-t-il donné de m'expliquer là-dessus si des explications m'apparaissent – ce qui n'est pas sûr. Je parle de la planète et, en cette planète, de ce lieu de douleur : ma patrie. Une patrie, et le possessif dont elle se fait devancer, voilà pour la communauté des hommes le leurre : *leur* patrie. Ceux-ci et ceux-là, comme c'est elle plutôt qui les possède ! Ceux-ci et ceux-là, gens de médiocre clan si inconvenablement affrontés que le photographe de l'éternité en a tiré parfois, pour sa délectation décorporée, des clichés indéfiniment superposables lors même que changent les acteurs et leurs couleurs. Philosophie courte en la matière, j'entends en celle-là où, par jeu et loterie, des hommes en leur entier sont

from Reading of a Woman (1987)

This destroyed land – these black roofs... The sea opposite: brilliant. A wounded angel moves through all of it and its powder of misfortune, and, in the dust, invisibly drags along its disabled wing. Would the angel be there to camouflage with flourish of metaphysical plumage the inexplicable unreason of things, their dislocatedness? And men, stirred up by forces they believe originate in themselves and thus are under their governance – mere puppets ardently borne up beneath the chandeliers of some theatre and bewitched by the limelight of a moment – here, men are already caught up by the reverse movement, here, disarmed, their prestige extinguished, they make way for the new crowd and its new gods moving towards nothingness. Thus do forces go. Only blind blind men believe in theories, in theorems, in that powerful bronze horse that, on public squares, bronze conquerors bestride. The world is but fragilities and frailnesses, and nature too in its least visibly naturate refinements, and man too with his daily bill of fare, and his wife. All that which is not made of bronze, but of lovely rainbow happiness, is subjected to the reign of forces, I mean, perhaps, the reign of the King's fools. And what if the King himself were mad? Thus ran my revery, over that dead man's land that was mine. And that I loved. The land to which the entire planet came suffering, out of compassion. For, as soon as I look away from Helena who knows and does not know she is observed, I, dead man, take up the entire planet in my absolute eye and, know it to be weak, and alive, and capable of transparency, I to whom knowledge has at last come.

That which I thus set forth, is mysterious, I fully recognise, and perhaps, subsequently, it will be given to me to explain myself in these matters if explanations appear to me – which isn't certain. I speak of the planet and, within this planet, of this place of pain: my homeland. A homeland, and the possessive which precedes it, are for the community of men what entices and deceives: *their* homeland! This group and that group, how it possesses *them* rather! This group and that, people of mediocre clan brought so inappropriately head to head that the photographer of eternity has at times, for his unbodied delight, taken endlessly superimposable snaps of them even though the actors and their colours may be changing. A limited philosophy in such matters, whereby, through gambling

enrôlés sous des bannières dont ils meurent; philosophie, oui, risiblement courte : la seule qui m'aille. La guerre, dit cet autre fou, n'a rien, n'a jamais rien prouvé – qui importât, et ce que l'une fit un jour, l'autre le jour suivant le défit. C'est fourmilière que tout cela, affairement, énervement d'insectes irrités et que les forces balayeront, que dis-je, sur qui, pour les disperser et à jamais les rendre vains, elles se contenteront, ces forces, une fois d'un peu souffler. Évanouies les armées et leurs dieux peinturlurés qui devant elles dansent et font mille cabrioles, ô petits soldats fascinés des causes perdues, et ternies les cuirasses et les causes, essoufflées les fanfares, quand arrive enfin l'heure exacte pour tout ce meccano de rentrer dans sa boîte, soufflent les forces ! et les passions deviennent buées sur la vitre des jours, et les terreurs. Pendez, désarticulés, petits soldats et petits chefs revêtus de soie à drapeaux, pendez à faire rire les enfants de toujours, hors des coffrets à joujoux qui vous retiennent qui par un bras qui par une jambe, l'instant sur vos simulacres de tombeaux étant de pauvre gloire inopérante. L'heure, après cette hécatombe, l'heure est au photographe. Puis, donc, que sourire peut consoler, consoler qui ? disons, par astuce des mots, que les hommes meurent pour des *clichés.*

Et pourtant, cette patrie, moi vivant, fut mienne – et ses pommiers. J'aimais, j'adorais respirer l'air haut tenu de cette terre, avec ses montagnes ridées comme une pomme, justement une pomme vieillie, et dont l'odeur fortifie, tout naïvement bonne, une étrange mélancolie d'avant l'automne, dans le bonheur des saisons. J'aimais, de l'air de cette patrie, le partage entre la terre et la mer, l'âcre parfum de chèvre fiancé non pas subtilement, d'ailleurs, mais rustiquement ou mieux : antiquement, à cette invisible vague cruellement alguée issue des remous de la très physique mer. Ô pays sous les pommes et les pêches et les raisins – et le charbon dans l'œil de tes femmes, en instance d'étincelle. Vos yeux, filles de cet ici-là, provocateurs comme des seins sous le lin apparus, parousie désirée par les anciens guetteurs des rivières – vos yeux, eux aussi de chèvre et de sel ... Ah, que j'ai désiré, sous les nuages et les trous bleus du temps, vos sexes noirs et longs, et sous la forme malhabile dont vous faisiez usage pour écarter, si mal vêtues étiez-vous, l'intensité directe allant à vos chairs compliquées et nues ! Patries, vous l'étiez, chacune de vous, mes femmes – patries de sable et de réalité exquisement liées, pour moi qui expérimentais ainsi, sous le terrible doux sein, l'existence d'un concret défini ayant nom identité, parfum opposable. Alors, sur tout cet éclatement, venait, fortement déployé, l'ange évoqué

and chance, men are wholly enlisted beneath banners leading to their death; yes, a ludicrously short-sighted philosophy: the only one that suits me. War, that other court jester said, has never proved anything – that mattered, and what one war did one day, another undid the following day. It's all a vast anthill, a bustling and nervousness of angry insects that forces will sweep away, that, what am I saying?, these same forces will be content to blow lightly upon, just once, to scatter them and render them forever futile. Vanished their armies and their painted gods dancing and prancing endlessly before them, oh little soldiers fascinated by lost causes, and tarnished are breast-plates and causes, and fanfares clean out of breath, when the precise moment comes for the whole meccano game to go back into its box, and forces blow! and passions mist over on the glass of days, and terrors too. Hang there, out of joint, little soldiers and little leaders clothed in flag-silk, hang there, causing the children of ever and ever to laugh away, sticking out of the toy chests just holding you in by an arm, by a leg, the moment upon your sham graves being of paltry, ineffectual glory. The hour, following this hecatomb, belongs to the photographer. Since, then, smiling may bring con-solation, but to whom?, let's say, through the artfulness of words, that men die for a *snap*.

And yet, that homeland, when I was alive, was mine – and its apple trees. I loved, I adored breathing in the high-grasped air of that land, with its mountains wrinkled like an apple, an aged apple, to be precise, and whose smell fortifies, in its simple goodness, a strange pre-autumnal melancholy, in the bliss of seasons. I loved, in the air of that homeland, the apportionment between earth and sea, the acrid scent of goats wedded not subtly, moreover, but in rustic or, better, ancient fashion, to the cruelly seaweedy invisible wave arisen from the eddyings of the most physical sea. Oh country beneath the apples and peaches and grapes – and the coal in the eye of your women, awaiting a spark. And the eyes of you, daughters of that hereness, provocative like breasts appeared under linen, parousia desired by the ancient watchers of rivers – your eyes, too, of goats and salt... Ah, how have I desired, beneath the clouds and the blue holes of time, your long, black sexes, and, beneath the awkward formality you were wont to use to fend off, so ill-clad were you, the direct intenseness communicated to your complex and naked flesh! Homelands you were, each of you, my women – homelands of sand and reality exquisitely bound together, for a man who thus was testing, beneath its *awful* soft bosom, the existence of something definitely concrete called identity, with its opposable scent. And so, above all

d'avant la blessure. Mais dégageons-nous de ces images : la totalité est abstraite et les morts n'embrassent, s'ils veulent être, que des totalités. S'ils veulent être véridiquement des morts.

*

Moi, mort particulier.

Moi – que tant de lambeaux encore habillent, qui ne sont point lambeaux de suaire... Et, dans ma transparence, voici que des objets me traversent, eux-mêmes transparents et qui sur eux maintiennent, on dirait, un semblant de couleur; objets, sentiments ? L'irisation, ne la dirait-on pas surgie de la tristesse en l'apatride, ici, au centre frémissant de quelle absence en quel céleste ciel ? Et, puisqu'elle s'éprouve soudainement observée, regardons, toute philosophie repliée soigneusement comme un mouchoir de soie sur une dent d'enfant, les agissements un peu vaporeux d'Héléna.

*

La nuit venait à peine de refroidir ses lampes et le jour s'habituait à naître. Le malaise de cette aube-là était grand. Héléna se dégagea de ses premières habitudes nocturnes, et des secondes, comme en saison le reptile abandonne, non sans difficulté, la vapeur d'une peau devenue vaine. Elle observa, immobile, dans le ciel du jour de noirs nuages, plus terribles encore de sembler doux. Elle était ce matin un cristal de songe. Sa tête, sa jolie tête de fainéante, était traversée d'incertitudes claires : c'est dire que ces incertitudes mêmes prenaient, fussent-elles blessantes, des miroitements. Elle alla, elle revint, de la salle de bains à sa chambre et jusqu'à la cuisine dorée de cuivres. Elle se fit, avec une eau tiédie, un thé sans âme. En elle l'âme soudain criait, foule immense. L'âme plus douce en elle que le sang d'après la joie. «Que m'arrive-t-il donc ?» C'était une frénésie, un déménagement, un quai de gare. Plus profondément le chant chantait, plus profondément encore son dieu dormait. «Quel dieu ?», dit-elle entre deux lambeaux de bruit dans ses oreilles, déchirées jusqu'en leur caverne vide. Plus profondément le chant chantait et le cœur vivant chavirait, d'Héléna, selon des parois lisses. Elle caressa à même le ventre, comme une mère ensoleillée l'enfant à naître, le silence en elle, ce dormeur.

this bursting and exploding, came, wings outstretched, the angel of whom I have spoken, the angel from before the hurt. But let us break free of these images: whole pictures are abstract and the dead, if they want to be, only embrace wholes. If they want to be truthfully dead.

*

I, dead individual.

I – clothed still in so many tatters, which are not winding-sheet tatters… And, in my transparency, objects begin to traverse me, they themselves transparent and maintaining upon themselves what one might call a semblance of colour; objects, feelings? Doesn't the iridescence seem to have arisen from sadness over statelessness, here, at the shuddering centre of what absence within what celestial sky? And, since she suddenly feels observed, let us gaze, all philosophy carefully folded away like a silk handkerchief around a child's tooth, upon the mildly vaporous antics of Helena.

*

Night had barely just cooled down its lamps and day was growing accustomed to birth. The uneasiness of that particular dawn was great. Helena slipped free of her primary nightly habits, and of those that are secondary, as in season the reptile sheds, not without difficulty, the fumes of a skin become futile. Motionless, she studied in the daylight sky black clouds, still more terrible for their seeming gentle. She was this morning a dream-like crystal. Her head, her pretty idler's head, was run through with bright uncertainties: these very uncertainties, that is, though hurtful, took on various sheens. She went back and forth, from the bathroom to her bedroom and even the kitchen gilded with brassware. She made herself, with lukewarm water, a soulless tea. Within, her soul suddenly cried out, like a vast throng. Her soul within, softer than blood after ecstasy. 'What is happening to me?' All was frenzy, wholesale removal, a station platform. The more deeply the song sang, the more deeply yet her god slept. 'What god?', she said between two tatters of noise in her ears ripped open to their empty cavity. The more deeply the song sang and Helena's living heart capsized, down sheer rock face. She stroked upon her very womb, like a sun-drenched mother her child to be born, the silence within her, sleeping away. Her eyes

Ses yeux allèrent à des objets. Certains, ce rose par exemple, elle se souvint de les avoir aimés. Ce rose, ô bibelot, ô moment frêle à l'ultime pointe du plaisir d'être, ô sommet de l'empire, himalaya sous le soyeux croissant, joliesse. Héléna se plut ainsi à légèrement divaguer. Elle divagua encore à voir ici telle plume de paon, là, porteuse d'étincellement, telle palme. Un mot se forma pour aussitôt disparaître sous l'ironique nuée : pureté. Ce mot reviendra au détour de ses routes, à l'embranchement de sentiers. Pure ? fus-je pure ? – et quand ? près des fontaines. Une ligne, une frontière a bougé comme l'ombre sur ses deux seins dénudés, un jour d'arbres. Elle avala un long moment de salive puis, pure ? impure ? se laissa couler, jambes pliées, sur des coussins. Pure ? impure ? Et moi, dis-je, mort ou vivant, à travers ces images surgies, apparitions ? Non, je n'interviendrai plus dans ta vie, mon amour, et comme la fable sortie de la mer et ses écharpes, à jamais sous ces mêmes écharpes je plonge. Héléna a l'une de ses jambes entortillée par jeu dans une écharpe qui, hasard, se trouvait là, et s'y trouve. Le temps est au présent.

Dehors, la ville agite de toutes les manières possibles les jouets de son brouhaha matinal. Matinalement elle avance vers son midi et son soir. Elle est tout ourdie de victoires et de défaites, toute tramée déjà et tenue en main par les uns et les autres. D'autres matins l'attendent, en succession. Jours et nuits lui feront, chacun à sa façon, au fil du temps, violence. La violence, noyau central de la vie, pulpeuse autour de ce caillou. Pierres (précieuses) sur les bras des femmes et à leur cou. Violence gelée par l'absolu, la vie parmi, charnellement... Héléna dégage sa jambe et son pied; à son cou, comme assouvissement et réponse, elle porte une main, la sienne, et tous ses doigts. Biche, elle est biche en ce silence. Car voici que tous les bruits sont partis. Tous, mais non celui-ci.

Un peu redressée sur le divan, elle regarde sa main retournée, retombée. Par terre, à même le tapis d'unie couleur, une fleur naît. D'où donc lui est venue cette couleur rouge qu'en elle profondément elle cachait avec avarice, pour vivre ? Tant de sang, Héléna, trésor de toi. Plus tard, tout à l'heure, l'on écrira dans des journaux qu'une femme belle et jeune s'est fait violence, on s'interrogera sur l'arme. Héléna, à l'instant présent, regarde avec surprise se faire et grandir très vite un géranium.

*

went to certain objects. Some, this pink one for example, she remembered having loved. This pink one, oh knick-knack, oh frail moment at the extreme tip of the pleasure of being, oh peak of empire, Himalayan summit beneath the silken crescent, prettiness. Thus did Helena take pleasure in the ramblings of her mind. She rambled on further, seeing now a certain peacock feather, now, bearing up some sparkling brilliancy, a palm. A word took shape immediately to disappear beneath ironical cloud: pureness. The word will recur at every bend in her roads, at every forking of paths. Pure? was I pure? – and when? by fountains. A line, a frontier shifted like the shadow upon her two bared breasts, on a day of trees. She swallowed down a long moment of saliva, then pure? impure? slid down, legs folded, onto cushions. Pure? impure? And I myself, I said, dead or alive, through these images surging forth, these apparitions? No, I shall not again intervene in your life, my love, and like the fable arisen from the sea and its furling scarves, forever do I plunge beneath these same scarves. One of Helena's legs is playfully caught in the twirls of a scarf that, perchance, was there, and is there now. Time is the present.

Outside, the city is rattling in every way it can the toys of her morning hubbub. In matinal fashion she moves on towards her noon and her evening. She is quite plaited with victories and defeats, well woven already and in the firm control of all and sundry. Other mornings await her, all lined up. Days and nights will, each in its own way, in the course of time, do violence to her. Violence, central kernel of life, itself pulpy about this pebble. Stones (precious ones) on the arms of women and about their necks. Violence frozen by the absolute, by life in the midst, carnally... Helena frees her leg and her foot; upon her neck, by way of satisfaction and answer, she places a hand, hers, and all her fingers. Doe, she is doe within this silence. For now all noise has gone. All, except for this.

Sitting up a little once more upon the couch, she gazes at her hand turned about, fallen now upon her lap. On the ground, right there within the single-hued carpet, a flower is born. But where has her red colour come from that deep within her she would avariciously hide away, in order to live? So much blood, Helena, a treasure of your own. Later, shortly, they will write in newspapers that a beautiful young woman did violence to herself, questions will be asked about the weapon. Helena, at this moment, is watching in surprise a geranium coming into being and quickly growing.

*

157

de L'autre côté brûlé du très pur (1992)

Et l'arbre et les fagots d'étincelles
Par centration du froid
Étreignant comme araignée le non-tenu
Où nous aimons en lente rotation
Le nu de jeune fille
En qui se forme de rosée l'inouïe parole
Comme une lampe embrumée s'abreuve

Et nous allons avec le bleu du gaz
De cette lampe étrange
Nous abîmer sous les cailloux qui brûlent
Rivage de lune indurée
Avec son liséré de braise, colombe
Faite pour notre amour, mon amour, faite d'un sens

*

Cette colombe avec le peu de braise
Elle est, ciel asséché, ma brûlure
Écrite au pourtour de l'arbre puis désécrite
Afin de laisser libre
L'esprit de qui l'illusion brille au ciel

Puis c'est sur l'arc et l'herbe
L'étoile en rêverie terrible, l'eau
Qui flambe avec la rosée des jardins
Debout façonnées en jarres leurs roses vides
Comme poupées de notre nuit mortelle
Attendant archaïquement le non-né

*

from The Burned Other Side of Purity (1992)

And the tree and the faggots of sparks
Through the cold's centration
Embracing like a spider the un-held
Wherein we love in slow rotation
The young girl's naked figure
Wherein speech unheard takes its dewy form
Like a misted lamp quenching its thirst

And we go forth with the gassy blueness
Of this strange lamp
To be engulfed beneath the burning pebbles
Shore of indurated moon
With its fringe of embers, dove
Made for our love, my love, made of a meaning

*

This dove with its few embers
Is, parched sky, a burning upon me
Written around the tree's circumference then unwritten
So as to leave free
The mind whose illusion shines bright in the sky

Then is upon the bow and the grass
The star in awful reverie, water
Blazing away with the dew of gardens
Their empty roses fashioned upright in great urns
Like dolls of our mortal night
Antiquatedly awaiting the unborn

*

L'enfant d'enfance est dans l'herbe; dans l'herbe
Il brille avec le jour
Il marche avec la lampe noire évasive
À la hanche du jour
Hache du temps où flambe aussi le jour
Et qui palpite où les nuages dorment

Absolue inchangée substance – le soleil
En lui poussière et lyre
Friable en son dessèchement de songe
Parmi les arbres qui verdoient sur la douleur
De cet enfant natal en perte pure

*

Beauté de ses orteils fruités de neige
De ce côté de la lumière où elle est statue
Étrange et brillante et morte un peu
Sous le froid des froids arbres, d'une larme
Endormis dans de la musique, violons cassés
Brûlant de cela qui fut : étranges feuilles
Gelées au revers du feu

        … Et tous ces nids !
Et tous ces corps dans les orangeraies !
Qui faiblement battent de l'aile au crépuscule
Comme au désastre de l'esprit le violent cœur
Vieilli sous un gémissement de tourterelle
De ce côté très pauvre de l'amour
En son odeur d'urine et de jasmin

*

The childhood child is in the grass; in the grass
He shines forth with the day
He walks with the evasive black lamp
At the hip of day
Axe of time where day blazes away
And quivering where clouds sleep

Absolute unchanged substance – the sun
Within him dust and lyre
Brittle in its withering of dream
Amongst the trees greening above the pain
Of this native child to no purpose

*

Beauty of her snow-fruited toes
This side of the light where she is a statue
Strange and bright-shining and dead a little
Beneath the cold of cold trees slipped with a tear
Into the sleep of music, broken violins
Burning away with that which was : strange leaves
Frozen on the other side of fire

           ... And all these nests !
And all these bodies in the orange groves !
That weakly flap about in the dusk
Like in the mind's disaster the violent heart
Grown old beneath the moaning of some turtle-dove
On this most poor side of love
Within its odour of urine and jasmine

*

Cette femme en son obscur visage
Aux tables de la neige
Ses longs violons brûlés jusqu'aux racines
Tout cela qu'elle regarde
Serrant le nom du jour entre ses jambes
Et le ruissellement de l'innomé
Le désir autour d'elle
Ô dents ô vieillissantes
Qui doucement luisez dans le terrible

Tout cela qu'elle regarde
Au point inimagé de l'esprit dans le jour
Ses mains ses mille mains et leurs phalanges
Distraites et sûres, sur le sexe noir de l'homme
Lui est dehors il chasse la lune et les loups il mange de la viande
Elle a entre les jambes un haillon rouge
Un baiser rouge et rouge
Elle est dehors aussi elle est dedans
La lampe de cela qu'elle est la mange
Anthropophage ô dévorant le non-physique
Son visage est de verre très fin quand il explose

*

Comme une grappe est déjà le vin comme est douleur
Le bleu regard voilé de la substance
De ce côté du jour où elles dorment
Les lampes les précieuses
De ce côté brûlé du très pur
Dans le retrait du souffle
Ce nu dénué d'être
Et qui s'en va d'un orteil léger de neige
Sous la lumière où tremble aussi l'oubli

À toute mère la prairie la plus légère
À l'aube en douleur pure
Comme une grappe est déjà le vin, comme elle pleure

*

This woman within her darkened face
On the tables of snow
Her long violins burned to the roots
All that she gazes upon
Pressing tight the name of day between her legs
And the streaming of the unnamed
Desire all about her
Oh teeth oh you who grow old
Gently gleaming in the terribleness

All that she gazes upon
At the unimaged point of the mind in day
Her hands her thousand hands and their phalanges
Absent and sure, upon the black sex of man
He is outside he hunts moon and wolves he eats meat
She has between her legs a red rag
A red and red kiss
She is outside too she is within
The lamp of that which she is devours her
Anthropophagous oh consuming the non-physical
Her face is of finest glass when it explodes

*

As a cluster of grapes is wine already as is pain
The veiled blue gaze of substance
This side of day where they sleep
Lamps precious lamps
On this burned side of purity
In the recess of breath
This naked figure devoid of being
Moving off snow-toed and nimble
Beneath the light where too oblivion trembles

To every mother the lightest meadow
At dawn in pure pain
As a cluster of grapes is wine already, as she weeps

*

...Et nous voici devant la mer comme une lampe
Entre nos doigts pulvérisée sous les nuages
Dans le temps courbe, entière absurde obscure lampe
En son désordre à qui s'éclairent des haillons
Pays d'ici, enfant de rose froide,
Où nous allons mourir de transparence
Brûlant d'une simplicité comme une neige

Où sommes-nous diurne ma divine
Plus simple que le simple simple fruit
Tombé près de la courbe mer, en jardin nu,
Dans le temps courbe, pieuse lampe, langue morte ?
Où sommes-nous, où sommes-nous, apparence,
Cette nuit où l'amour, lui seul, brûle nos nids ?

*

Et nu dans la dénudation, dans la
Dénudation est une lampe vive
Enracinée dans l'herbe près des larmes
Autour de son visage en nudité
Ô nudité de cette face obscure
Sous la lumière éparpillée de ses larmes

Et nous voici devant ces larmes de la nuit
Semblable couple de l'esprit dans la pensée
De la pensée devenue lampe vive
Enracinée dans le charbon de l'être
Qui est charbon de l'être et nuit vive
Brillant du crin terriblement nocturne
De l'esprit – en vérité cette femme
Assise dans l'esprit et désirant

*

... And we are here before the sea like a lamp
Reduced to powder between our fingers beneath the clouds
In curved time, entire absurd and dark lamp
In its disorder for which rags and tatters light up
A land here, a cold rose child,
Wherein we shall die of transparency
Burning with a simpleness like snow

Where are we diurnal woman divine
Simpler than the simple simple fruit
Fallen near the curved sea, like a naked garden,
In curved time, devout lamp, dead language?
Where are we, where are we, appearance,
In this night where love, alone, burns our nests?

*

And naked figure in denudation, in
Denudation is a living lamp
Rooted in the grass near the tears
Around its face in nudity
Oh nudity of this dark face
Beneath the scattered light of its tears

And we are here before the tears of night
Such a couple of the mind in the thought
Of thought become living lamp
Rooted in the coal of being
Which is coal of being and living night
Shining with the terrible night hair
Of the mind – truly this woman
Seated in mind and desiring

*

Cet enfant de l'esprit
Je l'ai voulu plus nu que le nu fleuve
En qui les époux dorment
Par l'herbe et la rosée de tous leurs membres
Jusqu'au plus loin du fleuve – table rouge
Leur couleur exilée pure et seule
Éclairant l'assemblée
Couple d'amants désirés des nuages
Dans la matière, attendant l'heure

Cet enfant de l'esprit
Le voici qui nous vient et nous revient
Sur lui soleil des larmes
Derrière les arbres on le voit puis on le perd puis il revient et meurt
Puis il revient par les chemins du cœur
Là même où nous voici tenus par la sécheresse
Nos doigts friables pluies
La barque du visage allant devant l'enfance
Le cœur, le cœur circoncis, attablé dans la privation

*

This child of the mind
I wanted more naked than the naked river
Within which man and wife sleep
Through the grass and the dew of their every limb
To the far reaches of the river – a red table
Their exiled pure and single colour
Lighting up the assembly
Two lovers desired of the clouds
In matter, waiting for the hour

This child of the mind
Comes back to us here time upon time
Upon him sun of tears
Behind the trees we see him then lose him then he returns and dies
Then returns along the paths of the heart
In the very place where drought holds us
Our fingers brittle rains
The boat of the face sailing by childhood
The heart, the circumcised heart, seated at the table of deprivation

*

Ce sein très pur au soleil accroché
Sera l'agneau de feu des montagnes
Corbeau de feu criant
Si dure épée dans la corbeille des montagnes
Hautes brûlant comme un rameau de neige
En l'amoureux été devenu songe
Sous le très noir couteau de tout ce vent

Femmes de fruits dans la lumière droite
Le cerf qui vous respire
Voici qu'il est en limpidité l'agneau
Au sommet des montagnes
Avec ses jambes filles
Ses jambes de blessure à peine filles
Par inversion du feu parfois colombes
Éparpillant leur gorge

Éparpillant la perle de leur gorge

Femmes de fruits avec vos conques filles
Et dans vos doigts comme une odeur de menthe
Corbeaux de vos seins purs
C'est de nouveau c'est de nouveau l'été de neige
Le chagrin froid des raisins nus

*

This most pure bosom clinging to the sun
Will be the lamb of fire of mountains
Raven of fire crying out
Sword so hard in the basket of mountains
Burning high like a bough of snow
In the loving summer become daydream
Beneath the most black knife of all this wind

Women of fruit in the straight light
The stag that breathes you in
Is here in limpidness the lamb
Upon the mountain tops
With its girlish legs
Its scarcely girlish legs of hurt
By fiery inversion sometimes doves
Fluttering away their throats

Fluttering away the pearls of their throats

Women of fruit with your girlish conches
And in your fingers a kind of mint smell
Ravens of your pure breasts
Once more once more it is summer of snow
The cold grief of naked grapes

*

Par le lié et le délié du souffle
Et ce théâtre en flammes
Ligneuse lampe vive
Avive l'ombre des colombes de la gorge
Car c'est théâtre, ce beau corps, ce labyrinthe
Formé fermé sur sa disparition
Les yeux – roses futures
D'une parole pure : aveuglée

Jardin de tout jardin
Sous la douceur cendreuse des colombes
En contre-jour de tout jardin brillant
Un jour de rosée folle
En contre-nu de tout le corps avant le nu
(Le nu terrible)
Et la brûlure de l'esprit jusqu'aux racines

*

Aux arbres de colombes
Sanglantes d'épée brève
Dans ce jardin de brusques fleurs mentales
Devenu tendre terre
Incorruptiblement dans les nuages
Et ce nu ciel d'étoiles
Leur crin entremêlé
Dormant dans la soie froide des nuages

Et notre amour ô mon amour est neige
Épouse morte vive
Comme une fleur à l'imbrûlée brûlure
Sur la table du rêve
Et le vent sur la table et l'arbre et l'excrément
(Forme de l'eau l'amande de ton ombre)
Ce soir ce soir rien n'est solide
Mais seulement
Ce croissant de lune et de fruits
Posé sur la nuit vive

*

By what is bound and unbound in breath
And this theatre in flames
Woody living lamp
Revive the shadow of the throat's doves
For this is theatre, this lovely body, this labyrinth
Created closed upon its disappearance
Eyes – future roses
Of some pure speech : blinded

Garden of every garden
Beneath the ashen gentleness of doves
Against the light of every garden shining
A day of wild dew
Against the nakedness of the whole body before nakedness
(Terrible nakedness)
And the burning of the mind to its roots

*

To trees of doves
Bleeding from brief sword
In this garden of sudden mental flowers
That has become tender earth
Incorruptibly in the clouds
And this naked sky of stars
Their manes intermingled
Sleeping in the cold silk of clouds

And our love oh my love is snow
Living dead wife
Like a flower with its unburned burning
Upon the table of dream
And the wind upon the table and the tree and excrement
(The water's form the almond of your shadow)
Tonight tonight nothing is solid
But just
This crescent of moon and fruit
Placed upon the living night

*

Son corps est une flûte de désir
Dans le jardin de l'épousée par neige
Sous la lucidité de ces noyers – la mer
Avec sa longue plaie de perles, les nuages
Dormant, conceptuels, dans les nuages

Et notre amour est neige
Comme est le fruit idée de froide lune
Sur les tables du rêve
Tables inachevées du questionnement
Et le vent sur la table et l'arbre et ce qui tremble :
La perle de substance, l'enfant de neige
Et le rien de la neige
Ce pur, ce très pur qui nous fonde :

(… Les anges le très nu du ciel les excréments)

*

La pluie est mélangée au lierre de substance
Sous la beauté de l'être et de la pluie
Aimé pays d'image morte vive
En qui l'esprit dans le réseau des neiges
Regarde se déconcerter l'esprit

                      ô patrie pure
Profonde es-tu, partie avec les arbres
Allés sur des cadastres d'incendie
Si beaux grands arbres dans leur verdoiement de cri
Plus pur que pur, leur cri, pavot des neiges
Par nuit de veille auprès de l'eau de neige
Fulgurant dans le brûlant jour de l'esprit

*

His body is a flute of desire
In the garden of woman wedded in snow
Beneath the clearness of these walnut trees – the sea
With its long wound of pearls, clouds
Sleeping, conceptual, in the clouds

And our love is snow
As fruit is idea of cold moon
Upon the tables of dream
The unfinished tables of questioning
And the wind upon the table and the tree and what is trembling :
The pearl of substance, the child of snow
And the nothingness of snow
This pureness, this great pureness that founds us :

(... Angels the sky's great nakedness excrement)

*

The rain is mixed with the ivy of substance
Beneath the beauty of being and rain
Loved land of living dead image
Within which the mind in the network of snows
Watches the mind in its disconcertment

                    Oh pure homeland
Deep are you, departed with the trees
Gone upon cadastres of fire
Such lovely tall trees in their greening cry
Purer than pure, their cry, snow poppy
In night of vigil by the water of snow
Flashing brilliant in the burning day of the mind

*

Et nous voici devant l'éblouissement
Éblouis par l'éblouissement
C'est peut-être la fin et c'est la fin
Cela, l'éclat des arbres,
L'éclat des arbres, le charbon de la blessure
Depuis l'eau la première
À laver cendre et rive, à consoler nos larmes

Le bleu du ciel avec l'enfermement
Et le soleil – qui du soleil parla ?
Les cils brûlés, nous contemplons la rivière
Ses eaux brûlées dans l'eau de la maison
Car c'est bientôt bientôt
Comme une main de jeune fille et de fontaine
La femme brune avec un châle d'eau
Plus nue, mirée d'éclat

*

«L'homme habite une maison de verre»
Et le violon de ce qu'il est est son triomphe
De larmes et de colombes
En relation de neige avec l'arbre
Cet arbre-ci privé de sa musique
Ses branches naturées sous le bâillon

Bâillon de neige sur les bouches de l'arbre
Aux invisibles branches
Déterrant d'une voix les fondations
De la maison de verre
Sous les aigles petits du très haut ciel
Mangeurs d'oiseaux, jeteurs de pierres
Se déployant dans la légèreté des archaïsmes

*

174

And we are here before the dazzlement
Dazzled by dazzlement
It is perhaps the end and it is the end
That, the splendour of trees
The splendour of trees, the coal of hurting
Since water the first
To wash ash and shore, to console our tears

The blue of the sky with confinement
And the sun – who of sun spoke?
Our eyelashes burnt, we gaze out over the river
Its waters burned in the water of the house
For soon soon she is
Like a young girl's fountain-hand
Dark-haired woman with her shawl of water
More naked, mirrored in splendour

*

'Man lives in a glass house'
And the violin of what he is is his triumph
Of tears and doves
In snowy relation to the tree
This very tree deprived of its music
Its naturate branches beneath the gag

Gag of snow upon the mouths of the tree
With its invisible branches
Digging up with a voice the foundations
Of the glass house
Beneath eagles small against the highest sky
Devourers of birds, casters of stones
Spreading wing in the lightness of archaisms

*

Déesses de l'été dans les nuages
Sur ce pays d'immenses immenses arbres
En des jardins posés près de la pluie
Comme un toucher soudain d'abeille froide
Femmes de lait avec les paysages
L'épée des larmes à la main ô invisibles
Au point le plus haut de l'été disparues
Au point le plus noir de l'esprit formées colombes

Et l'on salue l'ouverte lampe de colombe
Au point le plus haut de l'été disparu
Où les déesses de l'esprit sont des énigmes
Comme beauté songée dans le goudron
En attendant la réduction promise
Du nom qui est le nom derrière le nom
En qui s'effacera aussi le nom

*

La perle de substance dans la brume des arbres
Beauté est-elle et si creuse colombe
Absolue par l'éclat
Le ciel voilé de nids, vidé de nids, tous les
Nuages admis à des catégories limpides
Et retenant en eux l'ombre vide

Ô bonheur de non-vie
Jardin cerné de musique et de neige
Ô vie de vie ô bonheur de non-vie
Dans le léger flambeau que font les arbres
Autour du sein formé de la substance
Sainte colombe ouverte, entrouverte
Colombe avec le sang
Ainsi, tranché, que sein de femme

*

Goddesses of summer in the clouds
Above this land of vast vast trees
Within gardens placed alongside rain
Like a sudden touch from a cold bee
Women of milk with landscapes
The sword of tears in hand oh invisible ones
Disappeared at the highest point of summer
At the blackest point of the mind created doves

And we greet the open lamp of dove
At the highest point of disappeared summer
Where goddesses of the mind are enigmas
Like beauty dreamed up in tar
Awaiting the promised reduction
Of name which is name behind name
Within which name too will be erased

*

The pearl of substance in the mist of trees
Beauty it is and such hollow dove
Absolute through splendour
The sky veiled with nests, voided of nests, all
Clouds admitted to limpid categories
And keeping within them empty shadow

Oh bliss of no-life
A garden girdled by music and snow
Oh life of life oh bliss of no-life
In the soft torchlight made by trees
Around the formed bosom of substance
Holy dove open, half-opened
Dove with blood
Like woman's breast, sliced open

*

Que soit la pauvreté une très sombre fleur
Offerte par fatigue à toute nuit de neige
Suspendue au revers de l'être et d'un grand feu
Que porte en lui le feu du feu et le feu mange
Et nous le mangerons aussi sans pied ni main
Le feu seul! il crie à la neige : il veut
Qu'à lui seul le tout soit remis, le tout donné!

Et que donner sinon le don et que donner
Sinon la main, sinon le pied?
Ils sortent doucement de l'invisible
Tous deux, et qui vécurent, et qui d'amour aimèrent, et qui
                                        moururent...
Invisible est visible en eux et seulement
De lui et d'eux est seulement visible
La douce empreinte de grand lion dans l'invisible
Derrière un tremblement du feu, lui formé
De brume et de brume et de brume et de neige

*

Je suis au sein de l'être avec l'été
L'épée aussi de l'être dans l'aorte
La main palpant la table
Portant les fleurs, les fruits
Le tout suspendu à l'explosion

Au grand dehors de la maison de verre
Avant que descende la lune et que s'enfuie
L'esprit de lune au pur théâtre de l'esprit
Avec ses yeux de larmes :
On vient avec le lion
– Sa patte est enflammée par l'émeraude
À cause de son nom de lion dans le livre
De qui montent flammes très denses les rosiers
Puis ils retombent en sang

*

May poverty be a most dark flower
Offered through fatigue to every night of snow
Hanging on the other side of being and a great fire
Borne within by the fire of fire and fire devours
And we too shall devour it without foot or hand
Fire alone! shouting out to snow : wanting
Everything to be delivered over to it alone, everything given over!

And what is there to give except giving and what is there to give
Except the hand, except the foot?
Softly they step out of the invisible
Together, they who lived, and who with love loved, and who died...
Invisible is visible within them and only
Of it and them is only visible
The great soft lion's track in the invisible
Behind the fire's trembling, itself shaped
In mist and mist and mist and snow

*

I am in the bosom of being with summer
The sword too of being in my aorta
My hand feeling the table
Bearing up flowers, fruits
Everything hanging there upon the explosion

To the great outside of the glass house
Before the moon goes down and the moon spirit
Absconds in the pure theatre of the mind
With its eyes of tears :
They come with the lion
– Its paw is ablaze from the emerald-bird
Because of its lion's name in the book
From which rise up rose-bushes most dense flames
Then they fall back in blood

*

Le paysage est entré dans le visage
Comme une épée.
Ô larmes, larmes dans l'esprit, avivant
Une poussière immaculée de raisins purs
Le long de la route perdue qui fut impure,
Plus doux raisins sous la proximité des morts
Que larmes d'une antiquité profonde et pure

Ô pierre et qui es-tu, obscure pierre
De notre maison, qui es-tu, pierre de lune
Luisant sur la table du jour en partie double
Jusqu'aux montagnes de raisins sous les ramiers
– Terre profonde et pure et qui nous tue ?
Poussière est beauté de la femme et poussière
Est, face au froid, l'éclat ébloui de l'homme
Sa face adonnée au soleil, l'autre sombre
Passant au loin entre la vigne et les loups

*

The landscape has entered the face
Like a sword.
Oh tears, tears of the mind, quickening
An immaculate dust of pure grapes
Along the lost road that was impure,
Grapes more gentle beneath the nearness of the dead
Than tears of a deep and pure ancientness

Oh stone and who are you, obscure stone
Of our house, who are you, moonstone
Gleaming upon the table of day with its double entries
Down to the mountains of grapes beneath the wood-pigeons
– Deep and pure earth that yet kills us?
Dust is beauty of woman and dust
Is, before the cold, the dazzled splendour of man
Its face given over to the sun, its other dark
Passing in the distance between the vine and the wolves

*

de La terre avec l'oubli (1994)

Voici, rose de feu dans la brûlure,
Cela qui donne au feu sa nouaison
Quand l'eau est là, fille de la maison,
Et qu'elle veille avec le feu de la brûlure
Sur le toit et la longue palme des nuages
Allumée par le sang
Au-dessus de la rivière de l'oubli

*

Ô corps jamais perdu sous bien des nuits
Porteur en toi d'un incendie d'étoile
Qui est splendeur mouillant l'enfant des fleuves
Laissant dans l'air la trace de son feu
Et la voici de son époux l'épouse
Tous deux étant l'être soudain du rire
Et la douceur étant leur ange dans le rire
Face à ces grappes que leurs dents fortes dévorent
À même leur double corps devenu vin
Qu'ils boivent et boivent dans la grappe du sein

*

Voici la vie avec les chambres de ce monde
Et les palmiers qui souffrent dans le vent
Violons sont-ils dévorés de nuages
Et raccordés à la violence de l'esprit
Qui est le point de l'homme à la fin pur
Dans la lumière qui retombe et fait la lune
Toute vipère étant soleil et fruit

*

from **The Earth with Oblivion** (1994)

Here, rose of fire in the burning,
Is that which gives fire its knotting
When water is there, daughter of the house,
And when it watches with the fire of burning
Over the roof and the long palm of clouds
Lit by blood
Above the river of oblivion

*

Oh body never lost beneath many nights
Bearer within of a starry inferno
That is splendour moistening the child of rivers
Leaving upon the air the trace of its fire
And here she is spouse of her spouse
Both in the sudden being of laughter
And softness being their angel in laughter
Before these clusters of fruit their teeth devour
In their wedded body become wine
That they drink and drink from the clustering bosom

*

Here is life with the chambers of this world
And the palm trees suffering in the wind
Are they violins devoured by clouds
And coupled to the violence of the spirit
That is the point of man at last pure
In the light that falls moon-like
Every viper being sun and fruit

*

Nous sommes ici dans un pays qui rêve
Et toute femme éblouie de rosée
Avec ses bras très nus, avec l'air
Avec la lampe, avec cela au ras de l'herbe
Et toute femme éblouie et qui s'avance
– Quand l'eau est là, fille de la maison –
Son œil en nous pleure une perle immense

*

Et l'homme est là, si vieux parmi ses chats
Et il pleure et rien ne le console
Ni le terrible orage en lui du songe
Ni la jeunesse de l'Isis de la lumière
Ni cette étoile de plein jour devenue fille
Et quelle étoile? Il n'a jamais connu son nom
Ange, il veille au milieu de ses chats

*

A-t-il un nom lui-même? Il est un songe
Il est l'enfant de plusieurs vies et d'une mère
Elle est sortie de la maison elle est rivière
Celle en qui tremblent les flambeaux de la maison
Plus pure es-tu que le plus pur en nous, ô mère
Ô jeune mère de cet homme à vieux genoux
Et qui supplie ta main et tes genoux

*

Deuil sur cet homme et deuil, et deuil, et deuil
Sur tout cet homme avec son sexe de violence!
Il habita les chambres de ce monde
Et sa douleur fut grande d'habiter
Dans ce pays privé de ses rivières
Où toute étoile abandonnait ses champs
Pour le livrer à des rudesses d'ange

*

184

We are here in a land that dreams
And every woman dew-dazzled
With her most naked arms, with the air
With the lamp, with that amongst the grass
And every woman dazzled and stepping forward
– When water is there, daughter of the house –
Her eye within us weeps an immense pearl

*

And man is there, so old amongst his cats
And he weeps and nothing comforts him
Neither the terrible storm within of dream
Nor the youth of Isis of light
Nor the daylight star become daughter
And what star? He has never known its name
Angel, he keeps vigil in the midst of his cats

*

Has he a name himself? He is a daydream
He is the child of several lives and a mother
She has gone from home she is river
She within whom flicker the torches of home
Purer are you than the purest within us, oh mother
Oh young mother of this old-kneed man
And who begs for your hand and your knees

*

Sorrow upon this man and sorrow, and sorrow and sorrow
Upon all of this man with his sex of violence!
He dwelt within the rooms of this world
And his pain was great to dwell
In this land deprived of its rivers
Where every star abandoned his fields
Delivering him up to angelic coarseness

*

À la fin il dit : ange ! Il murmura
Le nom de l'ange de personne et s'endormit
Avec les fleuves, avec la femme nue
L'Isis qui fut sa mère et son enfant
Et son enfant jamais ne fut et nul enfant
Jamais ne vint lire avec lui le livre
Qui n'est le livre de personne un peu de vent

*

Et je salue la nudité de l'être
Si même il est parfois voilé de sang
Désir est-il dans la lumière songe
Si dévoilée qu'elle est la dévoilante
Et la plus nue qui n'est jamais la nue
La désirée qui n'est la désirante
Car elle garde sa peau sombre et elle refuse
De transformer l'entaille en transparence

*

Ô anges qui de nuit liez l'épaule
À l'ensemencement du blé funèbre
Donnez-moi seulement le blé de la parole
Que je le tende dans ma paume aux aigles forts
Ce blé mental formant leur nourriture
Il me permet de protéger ma proie
Ce cœur en moi qui est le fruit du songe

*

Deuil ! deuil ! deuil ! Oh, sur cet homme
Que tombe la rosée de deuil et de matin
Dans le matin d'aucun matin de rosée froide
Mais seulement c'est l'olivier du vent
Mais seulement est une lampe de démence
Qui se défait dans le sablonneux sable

*

Finally he said : angel! He whispered
The name of the angel of no one and fell asleep
With the rivers, with the naked woman
The Isis that was his mother and his child
And his child never was and no child
Ever came to read with him the book
That is the book of no one a stirring of wind

*

And I greet the nudity of being
If even it sometimes is veiled with blood
Desire is it in the daydream light
So unveiled she is the unveiler
And the most-naked that is never the bared one
The desired one never the one desiring
For she keeps her dark skin and refuses
To transform the gash into transparency

*

Oh angels that of nights bind the shoulder
To the sowing of funereal wheat
Give to me but the wheat of speech
That I may offer it in my palm to eagles of strength
Mental wheat forming their nourishment
Permitting me to protect my prey
This heart within me that is the fruit of dream

*

Sorrow! sorrow! sorrow! Oh, upon this man
May fall the dew of sorrowing and dawn
In the morning of no morning of cold dew
But merely is it the olive-tree of the wind
But merely is a lamp of dementia
That unravels in the sandy sand

*

Ô bien-aimée ! Il y a cet homme de substance
Abandonné par la parole et par les fruits
Il est dans le desséchement avec ses membres
Il attend ce qui va venir comme un cheval
Oublié dans le vaste jour de la prairie
Et le voici devenu vieux et le voici
Un homme assis dans la fatigue des membres

*

Ses mains s'en vont sans lui vers la brûlure
Pour caresser la femme inachevée
Entre elle et lui il y a l'épée des larmes
Femme elle va selon sa solitude
Comme une étoile éblouie par les prairies
D'où le cheval a disparu et seulement
Il y a il y a une rosée qui tombe
Il n'y a rien : la terre avec l'oubli

*

Oh beloved! There is this man of substance
Abandoned by speech and by fruits
He is in the withering with his limbs
He awaits what will come like a horse
Forgotten in the vast day of meadows
And here become old and here
A man sitting in the tiredness of limbs

*

His hands move off without him towards the burning
To caress the unfinished woman
Between her and him there is the sword of tears
Woman she goes according to her solitude
Like a star dazzled by the meadows
From where the horse has disappeared and merely
There is there is a dew that is settling
There is nothing : the earth with oblivion

*

de La nuit du cœur flambant (1994)

Sur les chemins de l'être et de la nuit
Il y a un arbre illuné par la lune
Arbre si seul et si d'antique terre
Qu'il dort ainsi que poupée endormie
Près des fontaines vives
Libres de vent dans la lumière nue

*

Libre de vent... ô biche de pensée
Sanglante aussi près de ce cœur qui rêve
Et rôde et rêve et sa lueur est pluie
En pluie tombée sur les dormantes choses
Très longues choses, roses désencombrées
Par le parfum de leur immense nuit
Qui, nue, sera aussi vêtue de nuit

*

Son enfant dans la mort
Depuis toujours il y eut son enfant dans la mort
Et le cahier de toute enfance brûle
Dans une chambre vive
Dans une chambre vide où l'on regarde
L'étrangeté du vide
L'absolu de l'étrangeté du vide
Avec, autour, la nudité des nuits

*

from Night of Flaming Heart (1994)

Upon the trails of being and night
There is a tree illumed by moon
Tree so alone and so of ancient earth
It sleeps like a doll asleep
By running fountains
Free of wind in the naked light

*

Free of wind... oh doe of thought
Bleeding too by this heart that dreams
And roams and dreams and its glimmering is rain
As rain fallen on sleeping things
Things most long, roses disencumbered
By the scent of their vast night
That, naked, will too be clothed in night

*

Her child in death
Forever there was her child in death
And the notebook of all childhood is burning
In a vivid room
In a voided room where we gaze
At the strangeness of the void
The absoluteness of the void's strangeness
With, around us, the bareness of nights

*

Ce lit le nôtre une guitare une eau longue
Terriblement entre les jambes de la nuit
Comme un corps simple est l'eau qui se défait
Et se refait en sa lueur d'étoile
S'en allant seule avec ses jambes filles
Sa touffe de violence et sa blessure
Ainsi que femme entre les nébuleuses
Allaitée par tous les chevaux de la nuit

«Nue, je serai vêtue d'étoiles», dit-elle

*

Ce soir elle a donné au rossignol
Son enfant son fils de toujours aimé toujours
Et rafraîchi de menthe immatérielle
Avec ses mains et la douceur de ses pieds nus
D'enfant qui doit mourir
Sous le plafond inexpliqué des nuits

*

This our bed a guitar a stretch of water
Terribly between the legs of the night
Like a single body is the water undone
And redone within its starry glimmering
Moving away alone with her girl-like legs
Her tuft of violence and her wound
Like woman amongst the nebulas
Suckled by all the horses of night

'Naked, I shall be clothed with stars,' she said

*

Tonight she gave to the nightingale
Her child her son of forever ever loved
And cooled by unsubstantial mint
With his hands and his bare feet
Of mortal child-like destiny
Beneath the unexplained roof of nights

*

Seize paroles voilées (1995)

1

Servantes de ma tête ô vous
Couronnées d'eau ô vous
Qui me donnez l'habit
Pour l'attentat contre les nœuds transparents

Je cherche les sanglots de vos joues noires
Dans ces buissons de feu. Je me souviens
D'avoir goûté la paix
Des pommes

Personne ne m'interdira plus d'entrer ici

2

Salut à l'aube vierge et mère
En fleur de fils
Sous un grain fin serré d'intuition

Qu'elle grandisse
Dans une robe noire
Soucieuse de l'éclat des soucis

Le front pierreux
Vers les directions
Et dans tout l'œil ce miracle
De larmes

3

Celui qui va – paix à ses griffes
L'enfant aveugle au grondement des roses
Son sang retourné par le fer

Son œil brûlant sur la bête à merci :
Les lions ont tenu son visage

Sixteen Veiled Words (1995)

1

Servants of my mind oh you
Crowned with water oh you
Who bestow upon me clothing
For the attack upon transparent knots

I search for the sobbings of your dark cheeks
In these bushes of fire. I remember
Having tasted the peace
Of apples

No one again will forbid me to enter this place

2

Greetings to virgin and mother dawn
Like a flower of sons
Beneath a fine close grain of intuition

May she grow tall
In a black robe
Careful of the bursting splendour of cares

Stony brow
Towards directions
And throughout the eye this miracle
Of tears

3

He who goes – peace to his claws
The child blind to the rumbling of roses
His blood turned by the knife

His burning eye upon the beast at mercy :
Lions have held his face

Un pied si mort sur l'étoile des barques
Et ces forêts disloquées par le silence
Ou : consolées ? Ses mains arrachent
Un fragment pur

Son cœur abrupt gouvernera le feu

4

Par qui ? je fus noué parmi les mers
Plus gravement que le bonheur en soi
– Et l'injustice active sur ma face

Ici nous bifurquons. L'amant des pierres
Emporte le rêve apeuré d'une pierre :
L'étoile d'une femme, ses jambes repliées

5

Je songe à l'osier de ses jambes
À ce fleuve entre elle et moi
Et je crie en maniant des outils

À cette ligne écrite et qui va disparaître
Avec son corps économisé pour
La seule rupture

Je songe à ses poignets devenus lampe
Et qui vont dormir au versant de la douleur

6

Forêt de l'araignée candide
Sœur de l'étoile désirante
Montre ta jambe de glacier

Sur une route d'arme blanche –
Le feu à tête d'oiseau brusque
Se déliera

Pour tisonner l'air interdit
Comme une folle bête fille
Son cœur amorcé sous les feuilles

196

One oh so dead foot upon the star of boats
And these forests dislocated by silence
Or : consoled? His hands tear free
A pure fragment

His abrupt heart will wield power over fire

4

By whom? I was knotted tight amid the seas
More gravely than happiness within itself
– And active injustice upon my face

Here we part ways. The lover of stones
Carries off the frightened dream of a stone :
A woman's star, her legs tucked away

5

I dream of the osier of her legs
Of the river between her and me
And I cry out as I wield implements

Of this line written and about to disappear
With her body saved up for
Sheer rupture

I dream of her wrists become lamp
That will sleep upon the slope of pain

6

Forest of candid spider
Sister of desiring star
Show your glacier leg

Upon a white-weaponed road –
The quick bird-headed fire
Will unbind itself

To stir up the forbidden air
Like a wild and foolish girl
Her heart primed beneath the leaves

7

(Je sors sous un grand jet pierreux)

(J'ai caché l'eau :)

(Pour un enfant doré)

Allant serrant
L'araignée fille et ange
Endormie dans la mort

8

Allant serrant
L'araignée fille et ange
Endormie dans la mort

Moi chauffé d'une rose
Dans une chambre étroite
Et sans issue

Autour grandit la dalle
Et des sanglots font retentir
Mes chiens

9

La mélancolie ailleurs rayonne

Comme le vin aux doigts de celle
Qui n'a ni corps ni ombre

Mais seulement la chambre d'une géométrie
    qui se consume

Donnant un angle
À l'oiseau gémissant

7

(I go forth beneath a great stony casting)

(I have hidden the water :)

(For a golden child)

Going forth holding tight
The spider at once girl-child and angel
Asleep in death

8

Going forth holding tight
The spider at once girl-child and angel
Asleep in death

I warmed by a rose
In a cramped room
With no way out

All about the stone slab grows
And sobbing makes my dogs
Howl away

9

Melancholy elsewhere beams out

Like wine upon the fingers of her
Who has neither body nor shadow

But only the chamber of a geometry
    being consumed

Giving an angle
To the moaning bird

10

Ô vin de la mélancolie
Tu m'as taché
Et voici sous toi les fragments de ma tête

(Les dieux) les croient de marbre. Ils sont
  de nerfs
Jusqu'à l'extrême étendue respirante

Serai-je admis parmi vous ô nocturnes ?
J'attends
Je suis les bœufs sous le ciel fin

11

La tardive la mal rentrée
Les bouquets lui font peur
Dans la maison très noire

D'où revient-elle avec ses doubles jambes ?
L'oiseau sanglant le dit dans la mort

Dans la grande pitié elle est assise

12

...Elle a des grappes. Elle
Donne un sein de bronze
Doux dans le monde et les vents comme
  un poulain

Son lait m'habille et me double
Et je vais fort d'avoir touché
Sa forme vide

10

Oh wine of melancholy
You have stained me
And here beneath you are the fragments of my head

(The gods) believe them to be of marble. They are
    of nerve and sinew
To the very farthest reach of breath

Will I be admitted amongst you oh nocturnal ones?
I wait
I follow the oxen beneath the delicate sky

11

She lingering she barely home
The bunches of flowers frighten her
In the most black house

Where has she been with her two sets of legs?
The bird bleeding tells us in death

In great pity she is seated

12

… She has clusters of fruit. She
Offers a bosom of bronze
As soft in the world and its winds as
    a foal

Her milk clothes and increases me
And I go forth strong for having touched
Her empty form

13

Limpide avant les barques
Doué de mort
L'occasion me rompra
Pour me soumettre
À l'eau frêle et sans ride

14

La lumière conservera le pauvre amour

Noyés d'astre solide
Nous dormirons sous les draps d'un peu
    d'ombre

Alors le froid du ciel recueillera
L'étoile fraîche de nos mains

15

Septembre brûlé de lis :
Dans la ville de neige noire
J'avance vers la chapelle de la Pure

Ailleurs me suivent
Dans une longue interminable fin d'été
Des têtes qui parlent
Peut-être de leur mort
– Limpide et voilée par le soir

16

Destin, et ces nœuds durs, ô bois
Décasqués aux portes capitales
Enfin tout ramassé dans les mouchoirs
Les pieds et les amours, les mains tenant
    le quoi
La ville aux têtes d'épingle, les rosées
    du nuage
Et nous – brûlés de paroles

*

13

Limpid before the time of boats
Gifted with death
The occasion will break me open
And subject me
To frail and unrippled water

14

Light will conserve poor love

Drowning upon our solid heavenly body
We shall sleep beneath the sheets of bare
    shadow

Then the sky's cold will gather up
The cool star of our hands

15

September burned with lilies :
In the city of black snow
I advance towards the chapel of She that is Pure

Elsewhere
In a long interminable summer's end
Heads follow me
Speaking perhaps of their death
– Limpid and veiled by the evening

16

Destiny, and these hard knots, oh woods
Unhelmeted at the capital gates
Finally gathered up in handkerchiefs
Feet and loves, hands holding
    the what
The pin-headed city, the dews
    of cloud
And us – burned with language

*

Éclats (1995)

Le blanc le noir le blanc
Ils ne sauront jamais
La couleur de notre âme

*

Le discours du nuage
Est un autre nuage
Leur silence est la pluie

*

Tout cela dans la brume
Les champs et les maisons
Les raisins les raisons

*

Tout marteau est léger
C'est la leçon
Du papillon qui rêve

*

Retirez le soleil
L'autre lumière
Enferme ses corbeaux

*

Miroir dans le jardin
Les fleurs soudain
Sont femmes

*

La lumière est de face
Et toi
Les cils baissés

*

Splinters of Light (1995)

White black white
Will never know
The colour of our souls

*

The cloud's discourse
Is another cloud
Their silence is rain

*

Everything there in the mist
The fields and the houses
Grapes mindscapes

*

Every hammer is weightless
Is the lesson
Of the dreaming butterfly

*

Take away the sun
The other light
Contains its ravens

*

Mirror in the garden
The flowers suddenly
Are women

*

The light is face on
And you
With lowered lashes

*

Son nom de libellule
Au ras de la lumière
Un brûlant hiéroglyphe

*

Immense est la montagne
L'oiseau la respire
Et l'efface

*

Ensemble femme et lampe
L'obscur le clair
Se sont mis à parler

*

Jasmin du crépuscule
La lampe attend qu'il brille
Pour odorer

*

Incendie du matin
Le réveillé
Doit cacher son aveugle

*

La chaise un peu partout
Assise dans les chambres
Attend que la mort se fatigue

*

L'arbre que j'aime
Est l'enfant de mon jardin
Ma tombe est sa fille adoucie

*

Its name dragonfly
Down amongst the light
A burning hieroglyph

*

Vast is the mountain
The bird breathes it in
And erases it

*

Together woman and lamp
The dark the bright
Have begun to speak

*

Dusk's jasmine
The lamp waits for it to shine forth
So as to smell sweetly

*

Morning's conflagration
Things awakened
Must hide away their blindness

*

The chair more or less everywhere
Sitting in rooms
Waits for death to grow tired

*

The tree I love
Is the child of my garden
My grave is its gentler daughter

*

Jardin de l'Un (1995)

Il faut l'escargot il faut le liseron
Il faut le froid feuillage et sa rosée
Les murs aussi posés dans la lumière
Et le tissage de nos mains dans la lumière
Sous l'angle dessiné et blanc des amandiers
Où dorment un peu nos impasses – tout cela
Notre respiration
Qui va dans l'infini se nuire et nous dissoudre

Ici je suis. «La lune est mon enfant» (la lune?)
Comme cela fut dit
Ma toute nuit si tendre par l'éclat
Très doucement mon épouse, ma fille
Dans ce lit de roches rompues, muscles noués
Lit de violence naturelle et draps du vent
Cirque de pierre malheureuse et conque fille
Sur qui passe et repasse
L'ombre du rapace inconnu de la mort

Voici enfin l'arrivée des nuages
En qui se fait et se défait la lampe fille
Déjà née de demain ô lampe rouge
En verticalité de jour nocturne
Sur la maison de feu des fous du rêve
Leurs draps tordus comme des nébuleuses
Leurs yeux délégation d'oiseaux vers le centre

Ma fille ma colombe
À toi de toi par toi l'étranglement
Cette lampe de givre
Toi-même à demi dénudée sous la feuille,
De ce jardin de l'Un
Où va ta nuit aimer ta transparence
Mille fois mon cœur cela brille
Cicatrice incicatrisable et qui palpite
À toi de toi par toi l'étranglement
Sous bien de pluie tombée
En qui sommeil avec le soleil nous dormons

Garden of the One (1995)

The snail is needed the convolvulus is needed
Cold foliage and its dew are needed
Walls too standing in the light
And the weaving of our hands in the light
Beneath the drawn white angle of almond trees
Where our blind alleys catch some sleep – all of this
Our breathing
That will in infinity wreak injury upon itself and dissolve us

I am here. 'The moon is my child' (the moon?)
As it was said
My full night so delicate in its splendour
Most gently my spouse, my daughter
In this bed of broken rocks, muscles knotted
Bed of natural violence and sheets of the wind
Amphitheatre of misfortuned stone and girlish conch
Over which death's unknown bird of prey
Flies to and fro

Here at last come the clouds
Within which the girlish lamp is made and unmade
Born already of tomorrow oh red lamp
Rising high from nocturnal day
Above the fiery house of those crazed with dream
Their sheets twisted about like nebulas
Their eyes a delegation of birds heading for the centre

My daughter my dove
To you from you through you strangling
This lamp of frost
Yourself stripped half-bare beneath the leaf,
From this garden of the One
Where your night will love your transparency
A thousand times my heart things shine forth
A scar that will not heal and quivers on
To you from you through you strangling
Beneath much fallen rain
Within which sleep with sun we slumber

Flambeaux de la rivière (1995)

Soleil si peu traversé de nos larmes
Pour toi nous avons déplié nos plis
Et nous voici à l'orée des nuages
Transparents sous la multiplication des nids
Et nous voici perdus peut-être et nous voici
Mêlés par vide au ciel des purs rapaces
Et la parole en nous est revenue

Frères voici le pain sous la musique
Et toute rose est sur la table : la voici
Rose sans doute enfin métaphysique
Et les bois du rossignol sont dans la chambre
Comme un peuple de verre
Dont je salue infiniment les ombres
Ployées dans les bras douloureux de la terre
Arbres mes arbres nous avons aimé la terre
En grands flambeaux avec ses branches de rivière
Dans ce pays d'allégorie venteuse
Où toute brume avec nous a disparu

Soleil ligne des larmes
Très pur soleil apprivoisé par les racines
Dans la brûlure et la dissipation promise
De l'étoile enfantine
À l'angle du détachement de la lumière
Rectangle impur découpé par ceci :
La chaise assise et le silence des joueurs
Obscur ici ouvrant sur la terrasse
De qui les sphinx sont nos fils dans la pierre

Torches of the River (1995)

Sun so rarely traversed by our tears
For you we have unfolded our folds
And here we are on the threshold of clouds
Transparent beneath the proliferation of nests
And here we are perhaps lost and here we are
Mingled out of voidness with the sky of pure birds of prey
And speech within us has returned

Brothers here is bread beneath music
And every rose is upon the table : here it is
A no doubt finally metaphysical rose
And the nightingale's woods are in the room
Like a people of glass
Whose shadows infinitely I greet
Bending low in the pained arms of the earth
Trees my trees we have loved the earth
Like great torches with its river branches
In this land of windy allegory
Where every mist with us has disappeared

Sun line of tears
Most pure sun tamed by roots
In the burning and the promised dissipation
Of the child star
At the angle of detachment from light
Impure rectangle carved out by this :
The sitting chair and the players' silence
Dark hereness opening upon the terrace
Whose sphinxes are our sons in stone

Bloodaxe Contemporary French Poets

Series Editors: **Timothy Mathews & Michael Worton**

FRENCH-ENGLISH BILINGUAL EDITIONS

'Bloodaxe's Contemporary French Poets series could not have arrived at a more opportune time, and I cannot remember any translation initiative in the past thirty years that has been more ambitious or more coherently planned in its attempt to bring French poetry across the Channel and the Atlantic. Under the editorship of Timothy Mathews and Michael Worton, the series has a clear format and an even clearer sense of mission' – MALCOLM BOWIE, *TLS*

YVES BONNEFOY
On the Motion and Immobility of Douve:
Du mouvement et de l'immobilité de Douve
Translated by Galway Kinnell. Introduction by Timothy Mathews.

Yves Bonnefoy is a central figure in post-war French culture. Born in 1923, he has had a lifelong fascination with the problems of translation. Language, for him, is a visceral, intensely material element in our existence, and yet the abstract quality of words distorts the immediate, material quality of our contact with the world.

This concern with what separates words from an essential truth hidden in objects involves him in wide-ranging philosophical and theological investigations of the spiritual and the sacred. But for all his intellectual drive and rigour, Bonnefoy's poetry is essentially of the concrete and the tangible, and addresses itself to our most familiar and intimate experiences of objects and of each other.

In his first book of poetry, published in France in 1953, Bonnefoy reflects on the value and mechanism of language in a series of short variations on the life and death of a much loved woman, Douve. In his introduction, Timothy Mathews shows how Bonnefoy's poetics are enmeshed with his philosophical, religious and critical thought.

Galway Kinnell is one of America's leading poets. His *Selected Poems* (1982) won the National Book Award and the Pulitzer Prize. A new *Selected Poems* is due from Bloodaxe in 2001.

RENÉ CHAR
The Dawn Breakers:
Les Matinaux
Edited & translated by Michael Worton

René Char (1907-88) is generally regarded as one of the most important modern French poets. Admired by Heidegger for the profundity of his poetic philosophy, he was also a hero of the French Resistance and in the 1960s a militant anti-nuclear protester.

Associated with the Surrealist movement for several years and a close friend of many painters – notably Braque, Giacometti and Picasso – he wrote poetry which miraculously, often challengingly, confronts the major 20th century moral, political and artistic concerns with a simplicity of vision and expression that owes much to the poet-philosophers of ancient Greece.

Les Matinaux (1947-49) is perhaps his greatest collection. Published after the War, it looks forward to a better and freer world, whilst also bearing the marks of a deep-seated hatred of all fascisms. It contains some of the most beautiful love poems ever written in French.

Michael Worton's translations convey the essence of Char's poetry (which says difficult things in a simple, traditional way), and his introduction suggests why Char is one of the vital voices of our age.

BLOODAXE CONTEMPORARY FRENCH POETS: 3

HENRI MICHAUX
Spaced, Displaced:
Déplacements Dégagements
Translated by David & Helen Constantine. Introduction by Peter Broome.

Henri Michaux (1899-1984) is one of the notable travellers of modern French poetry: not only to the Amazon and the Far East, but into the strange hinterland of his own inner space, the surprises and shocks of which he has never ceased to explore as a foreign country in their own right, and a language to be learned. Fired by the same explorer's appetite, he has delved into the realm of mescaline and other drugs, and his wartime poetry, part of a private "resistance" movement of extraordinary density and energy, has advertised his view of the poetic act as a form of exorcism.

His insatiable thirst for new artistic expressions of himself made him one of the most aggressive and disquieting of contemporary French painters. If he is close to anyone, it is to Klee and Pollock, but he was as much inspired by Oriental graphic arts.

Déplacements Dégagements (1985) has all the hallmarks of Michaux's most dynamic work: poetry testing itself dangerously at the frontiers, acutely analytical, linguistically versatile and full of surprising insights into previously undiscovered movements of the mind.

David Constantine is Fellow in German at the Queen's College, Oxford. He has published six books of poems and a novel with Bloodaxe, has translated poetry from French, Greek and German, and won the European Poetry Translation Prize for his *Selected Poems* of Friedrich Hölderlin. **Helen Constantine** has taught French at schools and polytechnics in Durham and Oxford. **Peter Broome** is Professor of French at Queen's University, Belfast. He is co-author of *The Appreciation of Modern French Poetry* and *An Anthology of Modern French Poetry* (CUP, 1976), and author of monographs on Michaux and Frénaud.

AIMÉ CÉSAIRE
Notebook of a Return to My Native Land:
Cahier d'un retour au pays natal
Translated by Mireille Rosello with Annie Pritchard
Introduction by Mireille Rosello

André Breton called Aimé Césaire's *Cahier* 'nothing less than the greatest lyrical monument of this time'. It is a seminal text in Surrealist, French and Black literatures, only now published in full in English for the first time.

Aimé Césaire was born in 1913 in Basse-Pointe, a village on the north coast of Martinique, a former French colony in the Caribbean (now an overseas département of France). His *Notebook of a Return to My Native Land* is the foundation stone of francophone Black literature: it is here that the word *Negritude* appeared for the first time. *Negritude* has come to mean the cultural, philosophical and political movement co-founded in Paris in the 1930s by three Black students from French colonies: the poets Léon-Gontran Damas from French Guiana; Léopold Senghor, later President of Senegal; and Aimé Césaire, who became a deputy in the French National Assembly for the Revolutionary Party of Martinique and was until very recently Mayor of Fort-de-France.

As a poet, Césaire believes in the revolutionary power of language, and in the *Notebook* he combines high literary French with Martinican colloquialisms, and archaic turns of phrase with dazzling new coinages. The result is a challenging and deeply moving poem on the theme of the future of the negro race which presents and enacts the poignant search for a Martinican identity. The *Notebook* opposes the ideology of colonialism by inventing a language that refuses assimilation to a dominant cultural norm, a language that teaches resistance and liberation.

Mireille Rosello lectures in French at Northwestern University, USA. Her books, all in French, include *Littérature et identité créole aux Antilles*, and studies of André Breton and Michel Tournier.

'Aimé Césaire's *Notebook of a Return to My Native Land* is one of the most extraordinary written this century...*Notebook* is a declaration of independence...As ambitious as Joyce, Césaire sets out to "forge the uncreated conscience" of his race...Rosello's introduction discusses the poem's influence on later Caribbean writers, many of whom have sought to close the gap between the literary and the vernacular that *Notebook* so vividly explores' – MARK FORD, *Guardian*

PHILIPPE JACCOTTET

Under Clouded Skies / Beauregard

Pensées sous les nuages / Beauregard

Translated by Mark Treharne & David Constantine
Introduction by Mark Treharne
Poetry Book Society Recommended Translation

Philippe Jaccottet's poetry is meditative, immediate and sensuous. It is rooted in the Drôme region of south-east France, which gives it a rich sense of place. This book brings together his reflections on landscape in the prose pieces of *Beauregard* (1981) and in the poems of *Under Clouded Skies* (1983), two thematically linked collections which are remarkable for their lyrical restraint and quiet power.

Jaccottet's poetry is largely grounded in landscape and the visual world, pursuing an anxious and persistent questioning of natural signs, meticulously conveyed in a syntax of great inventiveness. His work is animated by a fascination with the visible world from which he translates visual objects into verbal images and ultimately into figures of language. His poems are highly attentive, pushing the eye beyond what it sees, enacting a rich hesitation between meaning conferred and meaning withheld.

Born in Switzerland in 1925, Philippe Jaccottet is one of the most prominent figures of the immediate post-war generation of French poets. He has lived in France since 1953, working as a translator and freelance writer. As well as poetry, he has published prose writings, notebooks and critical essays. He is particularly well-known as a translator from German (Musil, Rilke, Mann, Hölderlin) but has also translated Homer, Plato, Ungaretti, Montale, Góngora and Mandelstam. He has won many distinguished prizes for his work both in France and elsewhere. His *Selected Poems*, translated by Derek Mahon, was published by Penguin in 1988.

Mark Treharne taught French at the University of Warwick until 1992. He has translated much of Jaccottet's prose and written on modern French Literature. **David Constantine** is Fellow in German at the Queen's College, Oxford. He has published six books of poems and a novel with Bloodaxe, has translated poetry from French, Greek and German, and won the European Poetry Translation Prize for his *Selected Poems* of Friedrich Hölderlin. The translators worked in close collaboration with Philippe Jaccottet on this edition.

PAUL ÉLUARD
Unbroken Poetry II
Poésie ininterrompue II
Translated by Gilbert Bowen
Introduction by Jill Lewis

Paul Éluard's poetry is concerned with sexual desire and the desire for social change. A central participant in Dada and in the Surrealist movement, Éluard joined the French Communist Party and worked actively in the Resistance in Nazi-occupied Paris. Caught between the horrors of Stalinism and post-war, right-wing anti-communism, his writing sustains an insistent vision of poetry as a multi-faceted weapon against injustice and oppression. For Éluard, poetry is a way of infiltrating the reader with greater emotional awareness of the social problems of the modern world.

Unbroken Poetry II, published posthumously in 1953, pays tribute to Dominique Éluard, with whom Paul spent the last years of his life. It traces the internal dialogues of a passionate relationship as well as of his continuing re-evaluation of the poetic project itself. It centres on political commitment and places it at the heart of the lovers' desire.

Gilbert Bowen's other translations include *Paul Éluard: Selected Poems* (John Calder, 1987). He died in 1996. **Jill Lewis** is Associate Professor of Literature and Feminist Studies at Hampshire College, Amherst, Massachusetts. She is co-author of *Common Differences: conflicts in black and white feminist perspectives*, and wrote a book on Paul Éluard entitled *Of Politics and Desire*.

ANDRÉ FRÉNAUD
Rome the Sorceress
La Sorcière de Rome
Translated by Keith Bosley. Introduction by Peter Broome.
Poetry Book Society Recommended Translation

First known for his war-time poems written from a German labour camp – notably his sombre reworkings of the myth of the Magi – André Frénaud (1907-1993) is one of the most searching of French poets. His work is structured by a sense of quest, which gives it its labyrinthine patterns, underground tensions and fractured, inventive forms. His poetry has an epic and tragic dimension: spurred by an urge for transcendence, it refuses false paradises, arrivals and notions of reconciliation.

Rome the Sorceress (1973) is Frénaud's richest and most disturbing confrontation with the hidden life of myths and the sacred, probing the themes of time, inheritance, revolt, illusions of divinity, father-figures, mother-figures, and the insatiable monuments of language which pretend to grapple with this weight of experience.

'Frénaud is a strong and original French poet who deserves to be much better known in this country. This book uses the city of Rome as a focus for an impassioned meditation on culture and barbarism, faiths and revolts, cruelties and aspirations. Pagan and Christian forces come alike under the burning-glass in a work of immediate impact, even if at times dark and enigmatic' – EDWIN MORGAN, *Poetry Book Society Bulletin.*

BLOODAXE CONTEMPORARY FRENCH POETS: 8

GÉRARD MACÉ
Wood Asleep
Bois dormant
Translated by David Kelley
Introduction by Jean-Pierre Richard

Gérard Macé's work challenges the barriers between poetry and the essay. This play between and within genres is essential to his writing – which has been called *essai merveilleux* – and derives from a questioning of language in its broadest sense. He is equally interested in the seductive musicality of words and in the remembered gestures which traced the hieroglyphs of Egypt and the calligraphic writing of the Far East. His fascination with dictionaries, grammars and glossaries leads him off on journeys in which the real and the imaginary are fused, but without being confused. He slips between words like a marvelling child constantly hoping that one day the world might be read like an open book.

This edition brings together three series of prose poems, *Le Jardin des langues* (1974), *Le balcon de Babel* (1977) and *Bois dormant* (1983). Other books by Macé have as their subject literary figures such as Rimbaud, Corbière, Nerval and Champollion, while *Rome et le firmament* and *Leçon de chinois* evoke places heavily charged with culture and history. His recent books include *Vies antérieures* (1991), which takes up the relationship between memory and writing, in the form of Lives (as in Lives of saints or illustrious men), and *La mémoire aime chasser dans le noir* (1993), which develops his fascination with the image – the poetic image, dream image and photographic image.

Gérard Macé was born in 1946, and teaches French literature in Paris. His *Leçon de chinois* (1981) is available in *The New French Poetry*. **David Kelley** co-edited *The New French Poetry* (1996) and translated Jean Tardieu's *The River Underground* (1991) for Bloodaxe. He died in 1999. **Jean-Pierre Richard** is one of Europe's foremost literary critics.

BLOODAXE CONTEMPORARY FRENCH POETS: 9
GUILLEVIC
Carnac
Translated by John Montague
Introduction by Stephen Romer

One of France's most important contemporary poets, Guillevic (1907-1997) was born in Carnac in Brittany, and although he never learned the Breton language, his personality is deeply marked by his feeling of oneness with his homeland. His poetry has a remarkable unity, driven by his desire to use words to bridge a tragic gulf between man and a harsh and often apparently hostile natural environment. For Guillevic, the purpose of poetry is to arouse the sense of Being. In this poetry of description – where entire landscapes are built up from short, intense texts – language is reduced to its essentials, as words are placed on the page 'like a dam against time'. When reading these poems, it is as if time is being stopped for man to find himself again.

Carnac (1961) marks the beginning of Guillevic's mature life as a poet. A single poem in several parts, it evokes the rocky, sea-bound, unfinished landscape of Brittany with its sacred objects and its great silent sense of waiting. The texts are brief but have a grave, meditative serenity, as the poet seeks to effect balance and to help us 'to make friends with nature' and to live in a universe which is chaotic and often frightening.

John Montague is one of Ireland's leading poets. He has published three books of poetry with Bloodaxe, and his *Collected Poems* with Gallery Press. He translated Francis Ponge's *Selected Poems* with C.K. Williams and Margaret Guiton (Wake Forest University Press, USA & Faber, UK). **Stephen Romer** is Maître de Conferences at the University of Tours, and published three collections, *Idols*, *Plato's Ladder* and *Tribute*, with OUP. He translated Jacques Dupin's *Selected Poems* with Paul Auster and David Shapiro (Wake Forest University Press, USA & Bloodaxe Books, UK).

Other French Editions from Bloodaxe

JACQUES DUPIN
Selected Poems
Translated by Paul Auster, Stephen Romer & David Shapiro

Jacques Dupin was born in 1927 in Privas in the Ardèche. Images of the harsh mineral nakedness of his native countryside run through the whole of his work and figure a fundamental existential nakedness. Dupin is an ascetic who likes the bare and the simple. His poetry is sad, wise and relentlessly honest. He speaks in our ear, as if at once close and far off, to tell us what we knew: 'Neither passion nor possession'.

He is a poet and art critic, and a formidable authority on the work of Miró and Giacometti. This edition of his prose poems and lyrics has been selected by Paul Auster from seven collections published between 1958 and 1982, culminating in his *Songs of Rescue*. It has an introduction by Mary Ann Caws, Professor of French at City University of New York.

PIERRE REVERDY
Selected Poems
Translated by John Ashbery, Mary Ann Caws & Patricia Terry
Edited by Timothy Bent & Germaine Brée

Pierre Reverdy (1889-1960) is one of the greatest and most influential figures in modern French poetry. He founded the journal *Nord-Sud* with Max Jacob and Guillaume Apollinaire, which drew together the first Surrealists. Associated with painters such as Picasso, Gris and Braque, he has been called a Cubist poet, for conventional structure is eliminated in his *poésie brut* ('raw poetry'), much as the painters cut away surface appearance to bring through the underlying forms. But Reverdy went beyond Cubist desolation to express a profound spiritual doubt and his sense of a mystery in the universe forever beyond his understanding.

André Breton hailed him in the first Surrealist Manifesto as 'the greatest poet of the time'. Louis Aragon said that for Breton, Soupault, Éluard and himself, Reverdy was 'our immediate elder, the exemplary poet'.

JEAN TARDIEU
The River Underground:
Selected Poems & Prose
Translated by David Kelley

The poetry of **Jean Tardieu** (1903-95) has an almost child-like simplicity, and in France his work is studied both in universities and in primary schools. Yet while he was a household name in France and has been translated into most European languages, his poetry remains little known in the English-speaking world, despite its immediacy and sense of fun.

In his early years the difficulties of writing lyric poetry in a schizophrenic age led Tardieu to a multiplication of poetic voices, and so to working for the stage, and he was writing what was subsequently dubbed 'Theatre of the Absurd' before Beckett's and Ionesco's plays had ever been performed.

This selection includes the sequence *Space and the Flute* (1958), which Tardieu wrote for drawings by his friend Pablo Picasso. Their poems and drawings are reproduced together in this edition, which spans 80 years of Tardieu's writing.

ALISTAIR ELLIOT
French Love Poems
Poetry Book Society Recommended Translation

French Love Poems is about the kinds of love that puzzle, delight and afflict us throughout our lives, from going on walks with an attractive cousin before Sunday dinner (Nerval) to indulging a granddaughter (Hugo). On the way there's the first yes from lips we love (Verlaine), a sky full of stars reflected fatally in Cleopatra's eyes (Heredia), lying awake waiting for your lover (Valéry), and the defeated toys of dead children (Gautier).

The selection covers five centuries, from Ronsard to Valéry. Other poets represented include Baudelaire, Mallarmé, Rimbaud, La Fontaine, Laforgue and Leconte de Lisle. The 35 poems, chosen by Alistair Elliot, are printed opposite his own highly skilful verse translations. There are also helpful notes on French verse technique and on points of obscurity.

THE NEW FRENCH POETRY
Edited & translated by
David Kelley & Jean Khalfa

This anthology captures the excitement of one of the most challenging developments in contemporary French writing, the new metaphysical poetry which has become an influential strand in recent French literature. It is a rigorously ontological poetry concerned with the very being of things, and with the nature of poetic language itself.

This is not the only kind of poetry being written in France today, but it is an extremely significant development, not only in French poetry, but also in French writing as a whole. Indeed, some of the writers included in this book, notably Édmond Jabès and Gérard Macé, have been influential in the subversion of conventional *genres,* by the play between poetry, narrative and essay, which has been an important aspect of recent French literature.

This anthology brings together writers of difference generations, from Gisèle Prassinos and Joyce Mansour, through Jacques Dupin and Bernard Noël, to Franck-André Jamme and André Velter. It represents those who are major figures in France and already have some reputation in Britain and America, alongside writers who are still relatively unknown to English readers. Much of the poetry shows an affinity with the work of Henri Michaux. The book also reflects the range of poetry published by the innovative French imprint Éditions Fata Morgana, as well as the lists of leading French publishers such as Gallimard, Éditions du Seuil and Mercure de France.

David Kelley was Senior Lecturer in French and Director of Studies in Modern Languages at Trinity College, Cambridge. He died in 1999. His books include his edition *The River Underground: Selected Poems & Prose* by Jean Tardieu (Bloodaxe Books, 1991), and a translation of Gérard Macé forthcoming in the Bloodaxe Contemporary French Poets series. **Jean Khalfa** is a distinguished French scholar and a former diplomat. He is currently a Fellow of Trinity College, Cambridge.

PAUL VALÉRY
La Jeune Parque
Translated by Alistair Elliot

'A poem should not mean, but be,' said Archibald MacLeish. *La Jeune Parque* ('the goddess of Fate as a young woman') certainly exists: she's beautiful and makes great gestures. And as for what she means, there's a substantial amount of argument about that, so *La Jeune Parque* is a poem by either definition. It's a classic, by general agreement, written to the full 17th-century recipe for alexandrine couplets, and it's modern, with every word pulling its weight in more than one direction.

Alistair Elliot's parallel translation with notes is aimed at making this rewarding but difficult long poem accessible enough for bafflement to turn into admiration. He attempts to clarify its small puzzles and also trace the overall narrative line of Paul Valéry's poem: it does have a story (what should a young woman do?) and does struggle towards a resolution. He also provides an introduction which deals with the interesting circumstances of the poem's four-year composition (1913-17), which resulted in Valery's instantly becoming a famous poet at the age of forty-five, after having written no poetry for twenty years.

This is Alistair Elliot's fifth book of verse translation – the others being Verlaine's *Femmes/Hombres* (Anvil), Heine's *The Lazarus Poems* (MidNAG/Carcanet), and *French Love Poems* and *Italian Landscape Poems* (both Bloodaxe). He has also edited a parallel-text version of Virgil's *Georgics* with Dryden's translation (MidNAG), and translated Euripides' *Medea*, the basis of Diana Rigg's prize-winning performances at the Almeida Theatre (1992) and elsewhere. His own Collected Poems, *My Country* (1989), and his latest collections *Turning the Stones* (1993) and *Facing Things* (1997), are published by Carcanet.